Spirited Imagination
Connecting With Your Spirituality

BY

Norman G. Middleton, M.S.W.

ISBN: 1-4033-0980-9 (Paperback)
ISBN: 1-4033-0979-5 (e-book)

This book is printed on acid free paper.

1stBooks – rev. 06/20/02

DEDICATION

THIS BOOK IS LOVINGLY DEDICATED TO MY SISTER, RAMONA, WHO TOOK ME TO MY FIRST MAGIC CAVE: THE CAPITOL THEATER, JACKSONVILLE, FLORIDA.

CONTENTS

ACKNOWLEDGMENTS

The author gratefully acknowledges permission to use material from the following sources:

Excerpts from THE JERUSALEM BIBLE, copyright © 1966 by Darton, Longman, & Todd. Ltd. And Doubleday, a division of Bantam Doubleday Dell Publishing Group, Inc. Reprinted by Permission.

Portions from "A Course in Miracles" copyright © 1975, Reprinted by Permission of the Foundation for Inner Peace, Inc., PO Box 598, Mill Valley, CA 94942.

CHAPTER ONE

Imagination and Spirituality

In fancy they pursue
The dream-child moving through a land
Of wonders wild and new,
In friendly chat with bird or beast-
And half believe it true.

- Lewis Carroll
Alice's Adventures in Wonderland

We've just begun a new millenium and most of us, like our predecessors, still don't get it. In a variety of ways we have been taught from an early age that there is only one reality, i.e. the material universe, but we don't get it.

The stuff we learn in church and Sunday school, from the world's great mythologies, from meditative states, and from our journeys within are given many names but reality isn't one of them. Freud thought all of that stuff was generated by wish fulfillment, delusion, neurosis, immaturity, and superstition. This did and does make sense to the scientifically disciplined, left cerebral hemispheres of many Twenty-first Century brains.

Why is it, then, so many of us can't shake off the notion that there is something more going on in life than that which is observable in the material universe? Efforts to collect evidence supporting this belief have not produced anything conclusive and, unquestionably, some of those among us who claim spiritual enlightenment are lunatics.

Why do we persist in the quest to discover the undiscoverable? Why has humankind persisted in this quest throughout history? Why have not the breathtaking illuminations of science settled the matter once and for all?

During my early years of treating people psychotherapeutically, I experienced myself as quite successful in helping them to overcome anxiety, depression, and other symptoms. In addition to this clinical effectiveness, however, there was a recurring theme among patients that I did not know how to address. Basically, the theme was a longing to find the "something more" in life which would make it richer and more meaningful. They believed the "something more" to be a non-material dimension that they could not quite grasp.

When confronted with this all-important issue, I sidestepped it by redirecting the patient to symptom alleviation, saying that feeling better would certainly make life better. Of course, there was some truth in this but I knew and the patient knew that the "something more" being sought was much more profound than feeling better. Unfortunately, it was one of many patient needs not covered in my clinical training.

Over a period of years as I devoted more time and energy to my own spiritual development, I became increasingly responsive to this kind of communication. Once I was willing to discuss the "something more" with my patients, I learned that the overwhelming majority of them were alluding to a spiritual connection that they felt they had early on but seemed to lose somewhere along the way. I began to search with them for ways to reestablish that connection. Our discoveries are the substance of this book.

Now, as I begin to commit what I have learned from this work to paper in order to share it with others, I realize I am inviting the others to take an excursion with me into a realm of mystery which, though fascinating, can be frustrating and sometimes frightening. It involves entering a realm where uncertainty reigns and our experience of the familiar is turned topsy-turvy. This may be a large part of why many prefer to dismiss it as "unreal" and unworthy of investigation.

I think the trip is worth my readers' time and energy because I, along with others, believe humankind is on the brink of its next great evolutionary breakthrough: a widespread recognition and acceptance of our basic spiritual nature and commitment to a life which gives it full expression. Homo sapiens (the wise man) is on the way to becoming Homo spiritualis.

We have come a long way with science and reason and many of us have believed that we would eventually find within their boundaries an explanation for everything. With this knowledge, we thought we could at last master our environment and ourselves. The forces acting upon us from both within and without would be fully identified and anything supernatural would have no relevance. Metaphysics would die a natural death.

The inborn spiritual component of the psyche never did buy into this and is now gaining ascendancy because it has become increasingly apparent, even to some of the most committed supporters of left brain rationalism, that science and technology are not making the world nor its inhabitants more understandable, better, or happier. People are still yearning for "something more."

No matter what we have been taught about the nature of reality, millions of us continue to imagine a non-material universe, a place composed not of things and creatures but of the essence of things and creatures - the spirit world. This realm is accessible only via the imagination.

Before proceeding, we are at a juncture where it is appropriate to spend some time reflecting on why we are endowed with the gift of imagining. We recognize imagination as an integral dimension of mind. Research confirms that it is a dimension that profoundly affects us physically and emotionally every day of our lives.

Images of people, things, and places that are not physically present are continuously popping into our awareness throughout our waking hours. At night in our dreams we are delighted, puzzled, soothed, and/or terrified by images of things no camera can record.

Our images exert a powerful force on our lives. It has been demonstrated that they can alter our physiological processes and our moods, inspire us creatively, guide us intuitively, contribute to life saving cures, and hasten death. There is evidence that they may affect our external environment as well.

Most of our imagery emanates from the right cerebral hemisphere of our bicameral brain, that 50% portion which is antithetical to the left hemisphere which is mostly verbal and dedicated to the principles of observation and rationality, the laws of cause and effect, and the physics of time and space. The right brain frequently and without apology presents us with material that is irrational and in violation of scientific "laws."

The foundation of evolution rests on the tenet that the universe supports that which is of greatest adaptational value to the species. Observing this, we must wonder why the right brain is alive and well in modern Homo sapiens. Why has it not withered with other useless appendages and attributes that evolved and failed to enhance survival?

Our right brain, filled with the stuff of which dreams are made, is grounded in symbols and metaphors rather than facts. To what end does it exist?

The principles of evolution say it must be good for something. It endures. It has not weakened over time. It must have survival value.

Well, its chief function is enabling us to relate to that which is not seen - that which is not verifiable through ordinary sensual perception. If nothing of the sort exists it would seem to be an unnecessary and even handicapping function.

Yet, if anything does exist which is not composed of matter, imagination is our single personal link to it. It may be that we are endowed with imagination because it is the only channel through which we can seek and know the "something more" which unceasingly tantalizes us.

Spiritual entities such as God ultimately can only be encountered in the imagination. No one has ever visited God and brought back a snapshot. Only in imagination can we give this entity some form or attributes to make it comprehensible.

This being the case, some people are drawn to the conclusion that God and other spirits are simply "made up" to fulfill a psychological need. This model posits that the imagination precedes and creates everything that is non-physical.

I invite you to consider the reverse. Start from the premise that independent spiritual entities do exist and that the imagination of those who reside in the flesh is the main or only channel these entities have for making themselves manifest or communicating with us.

From this perspective, imagination, rather than being a function of the mind/body system which confuses and misleads us, may be a God ordained faculty designed to assure our ongoing awareness of the "something more" which characterizes our experience of life on earth. Our persistence in imagining various spiritual beings, landscapes, and events may not stem from our need to satisfy some infantile wish but could be our reception of communication emanating from another reality.

If this is correct, we have a basis for learning to trust the imagination. It speaks the language of the soul (images, metaphors, poetry). If motivated to do so, the conscious Ego is capable of learning this language and can take part in soul journeys. To do so, the concession Ego must make is to accept that some of our images are psychic presences worthy of our attention and interaction. Carl Jung advised soul seekers to turn to their imagination.

The Early Connection Between Image and Spirit

We do not know at what exact moment in time humans became capable of creating images of things that were not immediately present or things that had no material existence at all. We do know that our earliest predecessors attached great meaning and importance to some of their images.

About 30,000 years ago our evolutionary ancestors began reproducing some of their images on the walls of caves. In France, Spain, and other places throughout the world, these cave paintings remain intact and are remarkably intelligible to citizens of the Twenty-first Century. Scholars have theorized and written much about these wonderful works of art and what they meant to those who created them.

We know the artists went to a great deal of trouble to paint or etch these representations on walls of rock. They had to work by lamplight, doing most of the work far inside the caverns in rooms difficult to reach. Some of them were accessible only via narrow crawl-through passages. Their placement tells us the artists performed their task in positions that were physically uncomfortable. The entire process involved personal discomfort and the expenditure of much time and energy.

What could have made such arduous work worthwhile to these early people?

Had the drawings been intended for adornment, they surely would have been placed close to the entrance of the cave so they might frequently be seen and appreciated by one and all. If they had been created for the private enjoyment of the entire clan, one would expect to find them in a living area.

Instead, the paintings were placed in obscure areas, suggesting the desire to limit visitation and, perhaps, to facilitate a ritualized approach to viewing them, such as having to crawl through a very narrow passage. This points to the likelihood that the paintings were regarded as sacred.

The rooms containing them are comparable to the modern chapel, a holy place. Joseph Campbell (1991) calls the caves in northern Spain and southern France "the great temple-caves," signifying their spiritual/mythological function. In these sequestered confines we discover the earliest known reproductions of our ancestors' imagery and find validation for the conclusion that they connected their images with things spiritual.

The images on the cave walls are predominantly depictions of animals, the food source of the people, their means of survival, fellow creatures with whom they had much in common in a kill or be killed daily existence.

The artists who created the drawings were emphasizing likeness but not realism. They apparently were not interested in producing the kind of work that might result from setting up an easel in the field and using live models. Their art was more purposeful than that.

They painted the image of the animal as it probably appeared to them in memories, dreams, and fantasies. Most likely, they wished to depict what they believed was the spirit or essence of the beast, "the idea of it" as Plato would say thousands of years later.

There must have been much psychological gratification in doing this. As they committed these spiritualized images to their stone canvases, they maintained complete control over them. This was an entirely different experience from their encounters during the hunt when they did combat with these powerful creatures in the flesh. On that turf, they were far from being the master. Their weapons were but sharpened sticks and there was a high probability they would be torn to shreds by their would-be prey.

Ah, but things were different in the cave painting room. Here, the animal spirits did the artists' bidding. They could and did group the images of the various species in ways that they would never have been observed in the wild. They could and did will the images to be in the throes of death or at the hunters' mercy.

No doubt, the paintings were capable of inspiring bravery and confidence in the hunters prior to their expeditions into the field. More importantly, they could be utilized in initiation rituals as youngsters left the status of boyhood and joined the ranks of the hunting men. Crawling through a narrow opening and tumbling into that holy space filled with animal spirits must have made novices breathlessly and suddenly aware of the spiritual connection between man and animal and the mystical dimension of the hunt.

Persons who were especially gifted at making drawings of the animal spirits probably came to be highly regarded by the clan. These were the individuals who could make the strongest spiritual connection with the animals. They could capture the essence of the beast and communicate with it. At some point the notion arose that this communication could be used to bargain with the animal spirits, even as a means of coaxing them to come to the hunt.

These spiritually gifted individuals became negotiators. They contracted with the animal spirits, getting them to agree to allow themselves to be sacrificed for the common good of the community in return for displays of reverence and honor in the sacred rituals of the clan.

The Rise of Shamanism

Those gifted in the process of imaging eventually were granted special status within the clan. The belief arose that successful hunting depended not strictly on physical strength and bravery but on skillful negotiation with the animal spirits as well. Who could do this better than one able to capture the soul of an animal in a reproduced image?

The belief arose that a gifted spiritualist could arrange a covenant with the animal to be hunted. The animal would allow itself to be slain and, in return, the clan would venerate it. Appreciation and reverence for the sacrificial beast were shown by having the spiritual leader don the skin, tail, horns, or other accoutrements associated with the animal and, in essence, become one with it, mimicking its

7

movements and sounds in a ritual dance performed for the edification of the entire group.

In this fashion, communion with the spirit of the food source was accomplished. The merging was total; animal and man became one.

Some of the cave drawings, most notably the one discovered at Trois Freres in France, depict someone carrying out just such a ritual. Dubbed by scholars "the Sorcerer of Trois Freres," this drawing is believed by many to be the first representation of a shaman. If so, he is the forerunner of a class of individuals destined to become recognized for having exceptional powers based largely on their talent for imaging.

This person may have performed the very first religious and magical rite. That was the transformation of human and animal into one being. There are indications that the shaman typically entered a hypnotic trance during the ritual, making it entirely possible that, upon return to ordinary consciousness, he truly believed the sacred animal had possessed him. He could vividly recall his journey to the land of the spirits accompanied by one or more animals acting as guides and protectors. He could recount in detail interactions with other spirits while abroad.

Moreover, the excited, equally entranced witnesses of the ritual no doubt responded hypnotically to the procedures. Watching the shadows cast by the fire and listening to the repetitive chanting or drumming that accompanied the dance invited them to enter the trance state along with the shaman, leaving them with the conviction that the shapeshifting was no illusion. For them, the shaman indeed had been transformed and transported to the spirit world. Afterward, when he told his story, they granted credibility to his account of what he had seen, heard, and done.

Shamans began to image frequent travels to the spirit world and perceived it to be much like the world of dreams. They found it inhabited not only by animals but also by the spirits of both deceased and living clan members, as well as by artifacts of the material universe. Rocks, plants, rivers, the sun and the moon were there, giving testimony to the fact that everything has a soul.

The spirits of the living found to be wandering about in this realm were believed to be there because their owners were sick or dysfunctional in some other way that caused the soul to leave the body. The shaman assumed the role of healer as he undertook to capture, bring back, and restore those souls to the proper owners.

On these journeys, shamans also encountered creatures and landscapes that had no earthly counterpart. They had run-ins with hostile entities that sometimes resulted in the shaman being torn apart and later having to be re-membered. The trips were dangerous and there was always the possibility that the shaman might not come back.

Upon coming out of the trance state, the shaman would relate to engrossed listeners what had transpired during his or her time in the spirit realm. The tales made it clear that the shaman was doing dangerous work important to the well being of each individual and the entire clan. Since the majority of the people were needed to hunt, gather, and perform the work necessary for physical survival, metaphysical matters became the sole responsibility of the shaman. Everyone in the social order depended on him or her to attend to the spirits. He was appointed master of ceremonies at regularly celebrated magical rites that allowed everyone to participate in his supernatural functions on a part-time basis without hampering their secular duties.

Magic, Religion and Science

As clans and tribes evolved into societies, the unique skills of the shamans were less in demand. At this level of sociological sophistication, spiritual connections became less important than environmental manipulation. In response to this need a new type of spiritual specialist emerged: the magician.

Reflecting vestiges of the shaman, the magician was looked to for healing and soothsaying. Though he might still utilize trance states for divining, excursions to the spirit realm gave way to more "educated" devices such as making predictions based on planetary alignments, reading the entrails of animal sacrifices, casting spells, prescribing amulets, etc.

It became standard procedure for sovereign leaders to consult with magicians on very important matters. At this level of decision making, it was essential that the adviser be unerring and more powerful than the magicians attending rival sovereigns. Those who were not were apt to become objects of the ruler's wrath and the executioner's ax. Conversely, those who displayed potency were usually handsomely rewarded.

The changing attitudes of the populous made demonstrations of power more important than imagery skills. Stories of travel in the spirit world were no longer impressive. People wanted more substantive evidence of magic at work.

So it was that the magicians of old found it necessary to create visible signs of their special power. It was also important that these signs be difficult to duplicate in case others might wish to challenge them for their job.

The magic recognized and utilized by the shaman, which was perceived to be a natural force woven into the tapestry of the universe and available to all who would seek it, was replaced. The magic of the wizard was a jealously guarded power possessed by a select few. More and more special effects were required to validate that power and, in this trend, we find the beginnings of the modern concept of the magician as an illusionist.

Concurrent with the rise of magic was the rise of institutional religion and, here, imagery found a repository though it was not as central as in shamanism. With the rise of religion, the old animal gods became more and more humanized. In many ancient religions the gods were part animal and part human until, finally, during the Greek and Roman eras, they took on the clear appearance of human beings, albeit super ones. Interestingly, even at this level, they frequently changed themselves into animal forms.

The shamanic communicator with the spirits was replaced by the priestly communicator with the gods. Trips to the non-material world gave way to ceremonies and ritual sacrifices through which the entire body of worshippers could communicate with the deities through prayer and sacrifice.

Imagery continued to be utilized in some individuals' programs of prayer and meditation. It was strongly favored by religious mystics who were seeking a personal revelation of the divine and those who could convincingly claim having had a mystical vision were looked upon with awe.

With the rise of Christianity and its obsession with the Devil as an entity roaming the world, intent upon luring mortals into sin and ultimate damnation, magicians as opposed to priests became increasingly suspect. Presumably, one could be sure that the priests' powers emanated from God but the magician might well be in alliance with the Evil One. It's a safe bet that the priests were among the most active promoters of this viewpoint.

Ironically, in time, the impeccable credentials of the priestly caste were destined to fall into disrepute as well. With the subsequent development and wide acceptance of the scientific method, the priest as well as the magician came to be viewed as misguided, superstitious, and unenlightened.

The idea of an unseen force guiding the universe was not acceptable to scientists. Once fully mapped out, the laws of physics were to be sufficient to explain all. The mission of the noble and objective scientist was to destroy the delusions of the past by uncovering new knowledge and interpreting it in the light of rational thought.

There was no need for either magic or gods anymore. The scientists proclaimed there was no such thing. The prominent place of the soul in healing was replaced by the concept of mind, defined as a function of the brain. Science was on its way to explaining all the mysteries of life.

The discipline of medicine arose, priding itself on its scientific underpinnings, and dedicated to arriving at a complete understanding of the human machine. Only in one remote corner of medicine did the machine and the soul continue to interface. This was in the field of psychiatry. Here, the imagination was too integral to the inner life to be discounted completely.

Psychology: The Death and Resurrection of Imagery

As the scientific method was applied to studying the workings of the mind, imagery had to be taken into account. Sigmund Freud, the father of psychoanalysis, recognized that the mental activities of infants and young children are formatted in imagery since the acquisition of language is a gradual process usually not even begun until about age two. Images are the only vehicle for mental life during our earliest period of development.

In pondering the nature of infantile imagery, Freud concluded that the earliest image we introject is that of the life-sustaining breast. Though initially we are not aware of to whom or what it is attached, he believed we soon associate the sight of the breast or bottle with the feeling of comfort and satiation that goes with being held and fed. When mother is unavailable, infants discover that it is possible to relieve hunger and tension by hallucinating the gratifying breast and the pleasant sensations it promises. In time that image comes to represent mother herself with all of her warmth, good smells, and pleasurable touch. At this point, the breast has become a true symbol.

You can see that, in Freud's framework, this earliest of images retains a magical component. Our infantile image has the magical power to alleviate our discomfort and provides us with immediate gratification. Though the image is not preferred over the physical presence of mother, it affords the baby sufficient pleasure to lead him/her to return to it again and again, especially when feeling deprived or stressed.

This model presupposes our knowing from our earliest days how to image and equally early acquisition of an awareness that images can alter our feeling states. As our childhood development continues, we collect an array of images that enable us to avoid discomfort and experience pleasure.

Freud went on to use imagery as a clinical tool until he devised the treatment method known as free association. Nevertheless, dream images remained a primary interest and much of his life work revolved around the analysis of dreams.

Carl Jung, the other giant of psychoanalysis, extensively utilized waking and dream images in his clinical work. Many of the examples of imagery work included in this book are variations of the technique Jung called Active Imagination. It was a mainstay of his therapeutic approach.

Like Freud, Jung believed that images express the content of the Personal Unconscious in the form of symbols but his model of imagery was broader. He posited that we come into the world imprinted with universal thought forms called archetypes.

These forms are an evolutionary inheritance, residing in what Jung called the Collective Unconscious, a repository of latent images originating in our ancestral past, human and prehuman. While not consciously remembered, archetypes create within us a predisposition to respond to the world just as our ancestors did. Thus, they are a compelling force in our life as we seek to replicate them in consciousness.

For example, the Mother Archetype is a blueprint of a mother that every baby seeks to flesh out as soon as life begins and is recognized in consciousness in the form of its actual mother. The preformed concept of mother is a determinant of how the baby will perceive its mother in the flesh.

We inherit archetypes from what Jung called the Collective Unconscious, the reservoir of wisdom and experience accumulated by our species through the ages. This information is transmitted within cultures through lore about religious figures and mythology. It is transmitted to individuals through some of our dreams and images. The important point here is that all of us have access to the Collective Unconscious. If we wish, we can learn to recognize and incorporate its material into our conscious life.

We shall return again to the ideas of Freud and Jung in the pages ahead. These remarkable men indelibly insinuated their theories into the field of psychology and their impact remains apparent today. Thanks largely to them, the much-maligned imagination retained a foothold in the realms of medicine and science.

Outside of psychoanalysis, imagery was renounced by mainstream psychology around the beginning of the Twentieth Century following John Watson's (1913) introduction of behaviorism. Watson insisted that psychology should address only observable and quantifiable dimensions of behavior in order to become an exact science. Thoughts, feelings, and images were declared to be irrelevant to the field. Anxious to attain the status of true scientists along with physicians, many psychologists embraced Watson's approach that excluded phenomena that were not amenable to laboratory observation and research.

For nearly fifty years, the main body of psychologists and psychotherapists made little use of imagery techniques. There was almost no research or published studies on the subject but when articles began to reappear in the professional literature people who were treating life-threatening diseases noticed them and began discovering imagery could have an impact on the natural healing processes of the body and its immune system. The result has been a somewhat reluctant rewarding of a place of respect to the human imagination as an effective agent in the practice of medicine.

Imagery, like the odious caterpillar, has emerged from its long night in the cocoon. Science itself has freed psyche to affiliate once again with the soul.

The Indestructible, Versatile Image

This brief history attests to the psychospiritual nature of imagery. This is why both science and religion have made use of it and have had problems with it. It is the area of interface between the mind/body and the soul. It is the means by which we integrate our worldly and otherworldly experience.

Neither the psychologists nor the priests can deny the power of the imagination but both continue to regard it as suspect. To the priest it is potentially a tool of the Devil and to the psychologist it is a troublesome phenomenon that validates the concept of spirituality.

Within the field of medicine, the healing properties of imagery are currently well established. Research supports that it can raise or lower our blood pressure. With it we can increase or slow down our heartbeat. We can cause our musculature to relax or grow rigid. There is also evidence that imagery can influence our blood clotting, the production of certain cells, and the release of natural chemicals within our bodies. Images constitute a kind of language that is understood and responded to by various elements of the mind/body system. No wonder it has become an almost standard adjunct to the medical treatment of serious illness and injury.

Psychotherapeutically, imagery is a prime modality for exploration of the psyche and a promoter of personal growth. It is an effective instrument for treating anxiety, depression, and other emotional disorders.

The main focus of the pages ahead is on imagery in another context. Just as imagery can open windows onto our Unconscious, it can open windows onto our spirituality and the realm from which it springs.

I know from my clinical practice that there are many people wishing to do this. They feel disconnected from things spiritual and some no longer can or desire to establish that connection through institutionalized religion.

Cataclysmic events tend to intensify the need for spiritual connection. The sad and horrifying attack on the Twin Towers on 9-11-01 has increased the number of spiritual seekers in my practice and, I daresay, all over the country.

In response to this need, I have included in this volume many examples taken from my case files which illustrate how a variety of individuals have managed to reconnect with their spitituality.

This material, disguised to protect patient confidentiality will validate that, although hardly anyone comes to therapy saying I want to connect with my spirituality, this is exactly what they are seeking. You will see how they and you can use imagination to that end and what can be discovered when you allow the spiritual part of you to instruct and direct you for at least a portion of your day or week. Chances are you have rarely if ever turned yourself over to that part of your being.

This book takes you on the adventure that ensues when you turn down the volume on your rational, scientifically oriented Ego and listen to the inner guide whose source lies elsewhere. It shows you how to develop a personal experience of the "something more" which transcends the material universe.

Now you have the call. The challenge is to allow your imagination, that frequently reviled human faculty, to lead you. We have been culturally conditioned to associate this faculty with madness, possession, immaturity, and a lack of grounding in reality. While none of this is true, most of us have a belief system in place that makes imaging feel like a risky, forbidden indulgence.

Nevertheless, our images can and will lead us to that ineffable "something more" which we sense is out there. It is a deep psychological and spiritual experience.

One of the metaphors often associated with the source of wisdom and guidance that dwells within us is the Wise Old Man. Carl Jung would call this an archetypal image, citing its repeated appearance through the ages in mythology and religion.

Alfred Tennyson displayed a fascination with this figure in the person of Merlin, King Arthur's teacher from childhood and the worker of many wonders. He is known to most of us as the Magician prominent in the poet's epic work, <u>The Idylls of the King</u>, (Tennyson, 1983).

Many are not aware that Tennyson did more work with the Merlin image long after his account of the events at Camelot was concluded. Just a few years before his death, he resurrected the great Magician in a poem entitled, "Merlin and the Gleam" (Tennyson, 1899).

In this work, he presents Merlin as a wise teacher and spiritual guide seeking to lead us on the quest for the Great Unknown. In the poem, Merlin addresses a young mariner who could be any of us. My call to you is echoed in his exhortation.

Launch your vessel,
And crowd your canvas,
And, ere it vanishes
Over the margin,
After it, follow it,
Follow the Gleam.

CHAPTER TWO

The Phenomena of Imagining

When people's eyes are open, they see landscapes in the outer world. When people's eyes are closed, they see landscapes with their mind's eye. People spend hours looking at outer landscapes, but there is just as much to see in inner landscapes. The landscapes are different, but they are equally valid.

- Mike Samuels, M.D. and Nancy Samuels
Seeing With the Mind's Eye

Imagination is our bridge to the realm of spirituality. Images are the products of the imagination. Therefore, we ask, "what exactly is an image?"

To my knowledge, no one knows or is even close to finding out. Plenty of research has been and is being done on the subject of imagery and most of it goes in one of two directions.

On the one hand, there are neurophysiological studies that are delineating the processes that must take place in our brain and nervous system in order to produce images. On the other hand, there are psychological studies that investigate what motivates us to image and the impact of our images on our mind/body system. The former thrust is likely to reveal to us how we image and the latter is likely to reveal why, but neither seems destined to tell us exactly what an image is.

Mardi Horowitz (1985) in his excellent book, <u>Image Formation and Psychotherapy</u>, tells us on the opening page that an image is a thought represented in a sensory mode. We shall rely on this as our working definition in the pages ahead.

While most of us are accustomed to thinking of images as visualizations, i.e. pictures in our head, Horowitz' definition recognizes that images often take the form of sounds, tastes, smells, touch, and kinesthetic sensations as well. A complete image may well incorporate all of the senses.

For example, a holistic image of a roller coaster ride would include not only the sight of the little cars moving along the serpentine tracks, but also the clickety-clack of the wheels and the screams of the passengers, the rush of the wind against your face, the smell of popcorn from the carnival concessions below, the taste of the hotdog you ate before getting on the ride, and the stomach-in-throat sensation during the dips. Images tend to be holistic whereas the observing rational mind tends to break things down into their component parts, analyzing each part separately.

Types of Images

An image that enters our consciousness can be welcome or unwelcome. A disturbing image might be an escapee from the Personal Unconscious where we store unwanted and unpleasant memories, thoughts, and desires.

It might be the result of some chemical action that is influencing our mind/body system. Alcohol and recreational drugs are a possibility and prescription medicines as well can affect us in this manner. Of course, chemically generated images can be quite agreeable to us and can be sought deliberately.

Various pathological states such as delirium and schizophrenia can also bring forth unbidden images. When they are particularly vivid and the imagist perceives them as originating in the external world rather than from within, we call them hallucinations.

Pain and physical or mental deprivations have long been known to invite an imagery experience. Shamans, mystics, and spiritual seekers have bequeathed to us detailed accounts of visions generated by isolating themselves, abstaining from sleep, exposing themselves to the elements, fasting, and inflicting pain on the body. Certain altered states of consciousness such as hypnotic trance open the gate to imagery experience while also rendering persons more vulnerable to having images imposed on them through the power of suggestion.

Most of our images are acceptable to us. Many are part and parcel of our thinking processes. We do a lot of our thinking in words but thinking is interlaced with sensory-based representations. Thinking about a distant loved one, for example, is often done by visualizing that person or sensorially reliving experiences with him/her.

Thought images are essential to certain problem solving tasks. When your car keys are missing, it's a safe bet that you will visualize or in some way get a sense of your movements and activities prior to the discovery of their absence. You will do something similar if you are asked to declare whether the green is at the top or bottom of a traffic light. The process will be like quickly reviewing an inner film clip of your encounters with traffic lights. This type of connection is made along a different route than the one you use to access who wrote Gone With the Wind or which city is the capitol of Japan.

In addition to our calling upon images for certain tasks, they spontaneously intrude into our consciousness many times a day. We might liken the imagery broadcasting system to a television channel that emits signals just about every hour of the day. If we wish, we can voluntarily tune into it but its signal, for various reasons, may reach our consciousness even when we are not seeking it. Most of us have been conditioned to quickly redirect our attention when this happens.

We can exercise a great deal of control over the imagery channel if we choose to do so. We can instruct it to create images of our choice and have them do our will. This is the essence of the daydream, a phenomenon with which we are all familiar.

Spirited imagining, the subject of this book, is a special way of imaging in which conscious control over the process is relinquished as much as possible. It is a process that calls upon us to set aside our usual notion that our images are "representations of something" in favor of regarding them as presences within our psyche. This is a profound change of viewpoint for most people, one we shall be expounding upon in the pages ahead.

The Limits and Liberties of Imagery

All of our perceptions throughout life are stored somewhere in our nervous system as images. Many of them are sooner or later translated into words that may also be stored but this is a secondary process. Images are the primary material by which our life experience is recorded within us.

In our culture, we emphasize the importance of verbal representations of what goes on in our psyches. On the plus side, words enable us to quickly transmit information to others and to receive in kind. The down side is that verbal transcriptions do not fully describe our sensory experience. This is what makes verbal communication shorter and more efficient. Images with all their subjective nuances can not be completely articulated.

We like to believe, as manifested by the value placed on eyewitness accounts in courts of law, that our recall of the events of our lives translated into words is a complete and accurate recapitulation. This cannot be so because they are incomplete accounts of what we perceive and our perceptions are partial to begin with. We can not at any moment be sensorially aware of everything occurring in our immediate external environment. Various psychosocial forces operate to focus our attention more intently on some aspect of what is happening while giving little notice to another aspect. When relating the events of our lives to others, our wish to convey completeness leads us, usually unconsciously, to fill in the gaps left by our partial awareness. In other words, we invent information that supports and validates our perceived fragments of what actually took place.

Nor are we immune from misperceptions based on which emotions, needs, and idiosyncrasies are in place at the moment of perception. If images, which are front line, are subject to this kind of distortion, think how much more warp can creep in during the translation of an image to the language mode? We are, indeed, as Shakespeare said, "such stuff as dreams are made on."

All of us recognize that some of our images are solely products of our imagination. I can image something that has never existed at all in the material world. I can image doing the impossible like flying without a plane. I can image being at some point in time long past or far into the future. The laws of physics or logic do not limit my imagination.

Most of us in childhood lived more in the imaginal world than the material one. Our early life was not restricted by someone else's definition of reality. In the process of growing up the definitions formulated by others were communicated to us with such authority that we discounted or renounced the imaginal world.

We were taught that imaginings were not to be believed, indulged in, or accorded respect. For the exploration at hand, we need to unlearn that. We must reassess the value of imagining. In doing so, you may rediscover a reservoir of beauty and wisdom that you have long forgotten.

Committing To Life Among the Images

A commitment is required if one wishes to consistently enjoy the healing and guiding benefits of the imagination. It entails a resolve to do more than just paying attention to imagery when it grabs you or you feel like it. It is a matter of living the imaginal life.

The commitment is to be aware of one's imagery on a daily basis and to interact with it. This means doing things with images like talking to them and listening for their answers, allowing them to take you on fantasy journeys, and creating rituals to invoke, honor, and encourage them. If that sounds kind of crazy to you, you're not exceptional.

My understanding and employment of imagery has evolved from my clinical work as a psychotherapist. My initial interest in it was as a tool for treating the various mental and emotional disorders which clients presented when they came to me for treatment. Many have said to me when I proposed interaction with their images, "I can't do that. It's too weird. That's the same as talking to yourself and everybody knows that's a sign of going around the twist."

My response is to agree with them. I say, "You know, you're right. I'm proposing that you work on your problem in an unconventional way. I can see you've applied conventional approaches and they obviously haven't been effective or you wouldn't be here.

"In imagery therapy, you'll be using your right brain more than your left. Like most of us, you've grown up thinking that this more imaginative, poetic side of your brain isn't good for much but I've found it to be a very potent healer. If doing a little crazy stuff will get you to feeling O.K., maybe it's worth it."

Not every client I see uses imagery and those who do achieve various levels of wellness but the majority tell me the process of imaging enriches their life and most declare an intention to continue their involvement with imagery after discharge. As a therapist, I find it to be the most exciting and productive of all treatment modalities.

Among the many benefits of imagery work, I discovered early on that it opened up to my clients and to me the spiritual dimension of their lives, an element that some therapeutic models leave out or suppress. It has brought home to me that the psyche and the soul are inseparable and that effective psychotherapy must be psychospiritual.

Imagination enfolds archetypal representations of the Divine and the essence of all created things. If allowed, these images will lead you on a path or paths that nurture your soul. The path may be one defined by traditional religions or it may turn out to be highly individualistic. Spirited imagination neither requires nor precludes allegiance to institutions.

At this point, an illustration from my files should be helpful. It demonstrates how the spiritual aspect of one young woman's problem was brought dramatically into her awareness as she worked with imagery to resolve what she thought was an unrelated problem.

Mildred's Incredible Cookie

Mildred was among the first clients with whom I did imagery work. She was in her mid-thirties and about twenty-five pounds overweight. She stated at the opening of our session that she disliked everything about herself.

Her weight was the focal point of her self-loathing and she especially berated herself for lacking the energy and will power to get rid of the extra pounds. Moreover, she felt that her career and social life were stagnant. She longed for a better job and more friends but was paralyzed when it came to action. She realized she was gloomy much of the time and believed her few friends merely tolerated her.

While this was Mildred's first foray into therapy, she had tried many self-help approaches prior to consulting me and "every dietary system in existence." She couldn't evaluate their effectiveness because she had aborted all of them in short order. In each case she could cite reasons for not continuing but in retrospect she viewed her excuses as contrivances. She supposed she just had no moral fiber.

This client appeared depressed and worn out. There was real desperation in her voice as she declared that she had to find something more in life to make it worth living. At this point, I asked her if she could recall ever having experienced life as an adventure or had a sense that some really wonderful things were happening in the world.

"Not since I was a little girl," she replied. It was a response quite familiar to me. Many people allude to their childhood years as a wonder filled time.

We discussed the probability that during childhood a part of her who saw life from a different perspective was operative. She remembered "just knowing" at an early age that magical things were going on in herself and her environment.

I informed her that in the course of growing up most of us learn to suppress the part of ourselves which knows about the magic. I told her this part was recoverable if she wished to expend some time and energy on reconnecting with it through her imagination. We agreed that doing so should enable her to engage more creatively in solving her problems.

At our next session, we spent some time discussing the therapeutic imagery process. I told her it was different than the way she might ordinarily image in that I did not want her to create any images. I wanted her to relax, take her time, and simply allow some image to come into her consciousness. The object was to employ as little conscious direction as possible.

I encouraged her to trust her Unconscious to send her an image that would be therapeutically useful even if at first it appeared to be silly or irrelevant. I stressed the importance of not judging or censoring.

At the end of our discussion, I taught Mildred a simple relaxation technique to which she responded well. While she was in her relaxed state, I asked her to submit a request to her Unconscious to send her an image that would help her to get in touch with that state of wonder that she had lost and wished to regain. Then, we waited quietly together for, perhaps, two minutes.

Eye movements beneath her closed lids told me when Mildred was in touch with an image. I also knew right away there was a problem because her brow became tightly furrowed and she let out a long sigh which culminated in a groan. Whatever it was, it was upsetting her.

"What are you in touch with?" I asked gently.

"This has got to be some kind of horrid joke!" she exclaimed. "I can't believe it."

Of course, it is desirable for the initial imagery experience to be positive. Negative images can be just as useful as positive but it takes some additional working through with the client to get there.

"No matter how bad it seems," I said, "please stay with it. Your Unconscious sent you this image for a reason."

"It's so awful," she said. "It's a cookie."

I could see tears flowing from her closed eyes as she continued. "It's my perpetual enemy. It's an Oreo."

I told Mildred I could understand her feeling of betrayal but affirmed my faith in the method that we were using. With my coaxing, she began engaging in dialogue with the cookie in order to find out more about it.

She reported that the cookie had a deep, soothing, male voice and that his name was, to no one's surprise, Oreo. He told her he represented the object of her deepest desire but added that she was confused about his true identity, which he would reveal later. He said that, if she were really serious about working on herself, he would meet with her again at her next therapy session. Then, he was abruptly gone.

Mildred returned to ordinary consciousness feeling angry. She couldn't comprehend how an image of an Oreo, the bane of her life, could be of any therapeutic value to her. She expressed misgivings about doing another imagery session.

At the end of the hour, I implored Mildred to have faith in the wisdom of her Unconscious and to allow it to lead her. As a home assignment, I suggested that, rather than avoiding the image, she would do well to gather all the information she could on Oreos. She replied sarcastically that she already knew all there was to know about them.

At our next meeting, I was surprised to learn that she had not totally rejected my suggestion. She had done a little homework on Oreos and found the result intriguing. For reasons she could not explain, she had begun to wonder if there was a legitimate word like "Oreo" and had gone to the dictionary. She did not find "Oreo" but she did find the word "orectic," which means something having the quality of stimulating appetite or desire - the opposite of an anorectic. This resonated with her cookie's statement that he represented the object of her deepest desire. It helped her to feel that something worthwhile might come from continuing her imagery work.

I once again guided the newly reassured Mildred through a relaxation procedure and asked her to call the cookie back into her awareness. He appeared promptly and the deep voice congratulated her for discovering with the help of the dictionary that his name signified his purpose in her life that was to stimulate her appetite.

When the client protested that appetite stimulation was the last thing she needed, Oreo told her to calm down and listen. "What you don't realize," he said, "is that I have come to stimulate your appetite for something more meaningful and nourishing than cookies and the other foods to which you are addicted."

Telling her to stay focused on him, he said he would reveal to her the thing she truly hungered for. He said she would see his cookie facade give way to his actual identity.

Mildred's expression was intense as she maintained silence for a few moments. Then, she appeared to have difficulty catching her breath and her facial muscles relaxed. She looked radiant.

My curiosity was over the top. "What is it?" I asked eagerly. "What do you see?"

Her voice was barely above a whisper. "The two wafers are falling off and the white center is growing large and bright. It's pulsating."

She was soon gasping audibly and pointing her index finger at the space in front of her still closed eyes. "It's an angel!" she exulted. "It's a beautiful angel dressed all in white."

From that point forward, Mildred had a partner in her therapeutic work and in her life outside of the therapeutic hour. She has continued to call him Oreo though he announced in his angelic form that his name is Oro (Latin for "I pray"). He has provided her with spiritual guidance, has helped her to explore her psyche, and somehow or another has helped her to lose weight. At the end of the year after their first meeting, she had dropped eighteen pounds with no stringent dieting or program and had accepted a new job in a career field that she found very attractive.

Oreo's mission in Mildred's life was to help her heal psychologically and spiritually. In fact, he brought home to both of us that the two dimensions are inseparable.

This is what Oreo revealed over a period of time.

He told the client he had been with her since early childhood and that it was he who had drawn her attention to the magic of the universe when she was a little girl. He was the energy behind those moments in which she had grasped a keen awareness of the divine, creative force behind everything.

Mildred expressed agreement when Oreo reminded her that she had pushed him out of her awareness by the time she reached puberty, though she was not aware of why she did. Oreo told her that he had remained with her in the dark side of her mind (the Unconscious).

While she consciously sought a feeling of fulfillment in ineffective ways, he had remained like buried gold waiting for her to unearth him and discover that what she really wanted and needed was spiritual fulfillment.

Gradually, Mildred and Oreo put together the dynamics behind their broken connection. She was the only child of parents who divorced when she was four. Her single mother who cared for her adequately, but was a depressed and cynical woman, raised her. Because she had been through painful experiences with organized religion during her own childhood, mother was fanatically opposed to acceptance of anything associated with religion or spirituality.

Mildred's childhood view of magic and things spiritual was severely squelched by this only parent whose support she dare not lose. Instead, she made a strong identification with her mother and paid no attention to spiritual urgings when they arose.

She almost reconnected with Oreo right after her mother's death when, all alone and in accordance with mother's wishes, she took her ashes on a dark stormy day to the jetties to commit them to the sea. On that bleak occasion she found herself shouting into the wind, "There must be something more; there must be something more." At that moment, Oreo was speaking to her. She listened briefly but cut him off once her mother's remains became one with the water.

Mildred decided she would try to find fulfillment through her secretarial career and a good relationship with a man. She also began turning more and more to food for gratification.

Over the next several years, she established herself as a top quality albeit joyless worker and put much effort into trying to make work two long-term relationships with men who treated her like an inferior. After the second, she found herself becoming depressed and cynical like her mother. This finally prompted her to seek help.

Oreo counseled that there are many spiritual paths and that this is a good thing because of our many individual differences. Her mother had closed down her own spiritual journey because she couldn't or wouldn't recognize that the traditional, organized church is not the only means by which one can seek the Divine.

He has led Mildred in growthful exploration of some of those alternatives. At my last contact with her, she was happily involved in Metaphysical Christianity though it may not be her end place. Many times, the spiritual search has no end place.

Who Was That Masked Man?

Oreo burst on the scene in Mildred's consciousness in disguise as a cookie. In imagery work, one becomes aware that images are not necessarily what they initially appear to be. The Lone Ranger is my favorite metaphor for this phenomenon.

The Lone Ranger endured as a radio show from 1933 to 1954 and also enjoyed a long run on television. The tremendously popular lead character embodied the attributes of both warrior and magician. Riding his supernaturally gifted horse, he disarmed people with magic silver bullets that never maimed or killed and traveled in brotherhood with his own shamanic, Native American Guide.

No one knew for sure from whence the Lone Ranger came or to where he disappeared. Many broadcasts ended with someone asking, "Who was that masked man?" His presence never failed to have an impact on others.

Although Oreo acquired an angelic face after initial contact, his features and costume were not the same during each encounter. A spirited image such as this is an archetype and can only take form metaphorically. It's true face can never be seen, only a series of masks.

Spirit guides represent a reservoir of energy and a psychic function existing within the imagist that is activated by a spiritual source. There is much more to them than what appears on the surface. Mildred's Oreo is a metaphor for that part of herself which is gifted to see the "something more" for which her soul was longing.

If we allow our images to be our psychospiritual guides, it is most important that we understand their metaphorical nature. To further clarify, consider how acceptable and even fashionable it has become for many individuals in our culture to entertain an image of their Inner Child. The concept of the entity within in us which we recognize as the Inner Child is largely unchanging in the particular feelings, attitudes, and behaviors it projects, yet the image it generates may never be the same two times in a row. Each of these changes may underscore a particular facet of the Inner Child archetype, deepening and expanding our understanding of the richness of its meaning but the image is not the thing. All of the images combined constitute a metaphor for a very real archetypal personality component that cannot be directly observed.

Mildred came to perceive her angel in this light. She concluded that his initial appearance as a cookie was his way of ensuring that he would not be easily dismissed. Had her first awareness of him been in his angelic form she would have found him immediately "unbelievable." His act of transformation helped her to see the connection between her conscious desire for goodies and the desire for psychospiritual fulfillment underlying that.

Surely, we can all agree that Oreo is a figment of Mildred's imagination but that is not sufficient cause to dismiss his significance. The force that generated this imagined form was healing and enlightening to her and profoundly affected her life. Her interaction with him led her to believe that, by projecting this image into her consciousness, her imagination had acted purposefully on her behalf to awaken her spirituality. Everyone with whom I have done imagery work has gained something of value from it when they related to their images as entities of meaning and not mere representations.

As Mildred embraced her image, she discovered symbolism embedded in it that left her in awe. Her contact with Oreo led to awareness that, in the cookie form, the dark chocolate wafers represented the encapsulating defenses she had used to contain and control the white spiritual stuff. As Oreo had suggested, she had been keeping her spirituality "in the dark." When the wafers' constricting hold was broken, the angelic figure could appear in fullness.

Simply by taking on the guise of an angel, Oreo was forcing Mildred to face the non-material universe. After all, angels are archetypal figures that have always been identified as otherworldly creatures that sometimes become active in the material world. By transforming himself from cookie to angel, Oreo left no room for doubt about where he would be leading his imagist.

Oreo is a spirited image, one of a class of images to which we shall give special attention in the pages ahead. His kind has been around for thousands of years.

Mildred has long since terminated therapy. At termination, she and Oreo were working so effectively on her problems that I had become superfluous.

CHAPTER THREE

In Search Of An Other Who Is You

"Don't you wish you were me? I know I do."

- Dudley Moore as Arthur Bach
ARTHUR (Orion Pictures, 1981)

Spirited imagination is imagination imbued with or directed by spirit. Not all of our imaginings are spiritually generated. Some are consciously directed inventions of the executive branch of our personality (the Ego). Some are representations of thoughts, feelings, needs, or wishes of another of the multiplicity of subselves that are parts of our personality structure. Psychological literature and popular self-help works have made these recognizable to us by assigning them names such as the Inner Child, the Warrior, the Lover, the Crazy One, the Angry One, etc. Many imaginings are admixtures of content from several of these components at once.

Lest you be alarmed by this assertion, let me remind you that we are not talking about abnormality. The human personality is not a unitary structure. The subselves to which I refer are clusters of attitudes, traits, desires, and behavior which hang together consistently enough to be recognized as free standing entities within the person.

They are entities which are not necessarily in agreement with or acceptable to each other. Their existence accounts for much of what we call our personal conflicts.

This does not mean that we all suffer from the psychiatric disorder that used to be called Multiple Personality and has been renamed Dissociative Identity Disorder. Although not as rare as once thought, this affliction is still not commonplace.

It is characterized by two or more distinct personalities dwelling within a single individual. Each has its own behavioral patterns and may become dominant, taking charge of the host individual at any moment in time. Eventually the controlling personality of the moment will be superceded by the emergence of another.

These appearances are not usually made at the request of and may not even be recognized by the executive personality. Rather, they tend to be sudden, unpredictable, and often extreme enough to be identified by observers. The executive component may be completely amnesic regarding what transpires when any one of the others is in control. When it regains ascendancy, it may be aware only of a time lapse.

While all of us share with Dissociative Identity Disorder sufferers the phenomenon of a divided self, those of us not afflicted with it are much more tightly integrated with our inner others and can exercise considerable control over them. We are, or at least have the potential to be, fully conscious of them.

One of You Is a Daimon

In the work at hand, we are chiefly concerned with the unique subself whose function is to connect us with the non-material universe - the invisible world which houses ancient wisdom, spirits, magic, miracles, and the Divine. It is this subself which connects mind with soul and soul with its source.

We are thinking here of spirit as the essence of being, the Divine element which is a timeless, totally interrelated, and unitary function. Soul is more personal, more closely tied to Ego, and progresses through developmental stages. The soul knows yearning and is nurtured by personal experience and archetypal influences.

Spirit is soul's guide and mentor. Soul is spirit's actualization in the individual being. Neither is visible but both can be experienced by Ego through imagination and emotion. Spirited imagination allows the interaction of soul and spirit to enter consciousness so that Ego can appreciate and participate in the high adventure of their travels together.

Spirit is a resident of both heaven and earth. It is a gift from the Divine that takes up residence within us. It is active in all spiritually rooted pursuits including creating, healing, transcending, and growing.

Manifestations of this principle at work can be found in the oracles of ancient Egypt, Rome, and other cultures. More familiar to most of us, it is manifest in the prophets of the Old Testament. All of these people perceived themselves to be directed by an indwelling supernatural entity.

The same was true for persons known as the wu in First Century China and for a number of rabbis in medieval times that were guided by a discarnate teacher called a maggid. Actually, the concept of soul and spirit interfacing can be traced all the way to the shamans of pre-history whose rites for enhancing the process are still viable.

The Ancient Greeks believed in invisible beings called Daimons which were spirits assigned by Zeus, king of the gods, to attend, protect, and guide persons, places, councils, and societies. The Daimon is my favorite representation of the spirit function. The Greeks perceived the Daimon to be a positive life force but recognized it could work for good or evil, be constructive or destructive, depending on how each individual related to it. The Daimon concept better lends itself to an understanding of the interactive bonding of mind and soul which is the focus of this book than the more traditional, theological word "spirit."

The Daimon was Zeus' supernatural gift to every mortal. It was endowed with the wisdom and creativity of the gods and totally committed to the well being of the one it served. It was to be that individual's personal, spiritual guide on his or her journey through life.

In Greek literature there are many references to this entity and the value placed on it. In Plato's (1942) <u>Apology</u>, the great philosopher Socrates alludes to his personal Daimon as a kind of voice which first came to him when he was a child and deterred him from becoming a politician. This is a good example of the Daimon speaking in a still, small voice from within, a function it has performed for kings, peasants, oracles, fools and geniuses throughout the ages.

The Daimon's gifts are not limited to this intuitive function. It is also an enabler. Through the imagination, it facilitates the soul's quest to become all that it is capable of being and to fulfill its ultimate destiny.

Nowhere can the magical work of the Daimon and its impact on personal development be more clearly observed than in the imaginative play of a child. The Daimonic Function drives and guides each child in the exploration of worlds beyond the material world in preparation for the spiritual quest which in time will be an essential aspect of what Jung called his or her individuation. Looking back on the experience of being a child to observe the workings of the Daimon is one of the best ways to begin reconnecting with it.

For example, I can access the feelings and behaviors associated with a long series of days when I was five years old. During most of that summer, my life settled into a sublime routine that usually started out with the consumption of a sugary slice of cinnamon toast made in the oven. It was accompanied by a steaming cup of sweetened coffee mixed in equal parts with Pet Milk poured directly from the can.

This bounty was consumed at an enamel-topped table in the kitchen while my mother sat beside me drinking her own morning coffee. I can still experience the smells, tastes, and feelings of those moments.

Though it was a warm and special time, the breakfast was only a prelude to the really great events of that period. In fact, I found it difficult to keep my attention on the food for very long.

The true glory of those days began as I exited through the screen door at the rear of the kitchen and emerged into a small, sparsely grassed backyard, which seemed boundless to me. It bordered on an alley just wide enough for the trash collection truck to pass through. It was my field of dreams, the fertile ground that spawned my daily transformation.

With twin, pearl handled pistols bearing Gene Autry's autograph holstered at my non-existent hips and a cowboy hat planted firmly on my head, I became for the next few hours my western movie hero of the day. Most often that would be either Johnny Mack Brown, Buck Jones, or William Boyd (known to me exclusively as Hopalong Cassidy).

Chases, fights, and shoot-outs were the order of the day as I took on an endless army of bad guys and kidded with my imaginary sidekicks. Occasionally, I even became one of the outlaws, which assured my being riddled with bullets in a short time.

The grown-ups called this activity "play" and I learned to use the same word for it. The popular meaning of "play" is an activity carried on for amusement. I now know the word only partially describes what I was doing in that summer of my sixth year.

During a large portion of those play periods I was completely detached from my own little kid identity. I actually became my version of the person I imagined Johnny Mack, Buck, or Hopalong to be. My acted-out attitudes and actions were different in each persona. The spirit of the chase varied depending on whether I was astride Reno, Silver, or Topper.

This was more than simple amusement. Though unaware of it, I was performing shamanic magic. I was shapeshifting, experiencing transformation.

From a psychological perspective, I was frequently in a trance state during my play periods, acting on self-suggestion. When I told myself I was Hopalong, for all practical purposes I was.

Much later, during my teens, I got my first view of a stage hypnotist at work. He gave a suggestion to a man from the audience, telling him he was a chicken. We all laughed uproariously as the entranced gentleman went about clucking, pecking, and turning red as a beet as he strained to lay an egg. Years later, I connected that demonstration with my childhood transformation into a cowboy and realized the two processes were essentially the same.

The astounding thing about all of this is that, at the tender age of five, I knew how to work big time magic. No training was required. The wizard within me had empowered me to be an accomplished self-hypnotist and shaman.

My powers were not limited to assuming different forms. I could make things appear and disappear as well. I could talk to animals and to invisible people. I could make things happen or not happen through my thoughts and actions. I could instantly relocate myself to any geographical area and could travel into the past or future with ease. I could be wounded and heal in an instant. I could die and be resurrected in a heartbeat.

My imagination was the most powerful force in my life and its uncritical acceptance of magic led me to believe that the entire universe was enchanted. My archetypal cowboy heroes were the first gods of my embryonic personal spirit world. They were to me immortal, infinitely good, heroic, and performers of wonders. They had power animals in their service. In time, I would see other faces of God but they were the progenitors of my first mythology; they were my first images of the Divine.

Amazingly, in just a few years, I unlearned my magical skills and denied the value of the power with which I had been endowed. At that point in my life, God was dead and would have to await his/her resurrection.

Hopefully, you can find in your own recall of early life experiences similar evidence of the Daimon's influence. Examine your "play" time in terms of how it might have been directing you and try to identify what kind of God or gods your Daimon was introducing to you.

Those of you of more recent generations may not have had much experience with the kind of play I am talking about. Unfortunately (my opinion) children are increasingly being engaged in highly structured activities requiring special equipment, technical skills, and adult input - all to the detriment of imaginative play. The Daimon is being snuffed out at earlier and earlier ages.

The Fate of the Daimon

In the best of all possible worlds, we would learn to value and continue to integrate what the Daimon teaches us about transcending the barriers of space, time, energy, and matter. At the same time, we would be developing and making use of our reasoning abilities toward establishing ourselves as rational beings in the material world. The concept of maturity would rest on the maintenance of a balance between these two dimensions of awareness, with neither being viewed as discrediting the other. Reality would be defined as a bifurcated realm encompassing the visible and invisible universes of which we are a part - separate but related realities governed by different laws.

The attainment of such a viewpoint upon reaching adulthood was not possible for me and probably not for you. It is a rare family in our culture that pays attention to or attaches value to its children's imaginings. When I was a child I often heard the big people say I had a vivid imagination but it was uttered in tones suggesting it was a condition on a par with chicken pox.

In school we are taught to crank up the left brain. In our scientific, technological society, lefty's workings are glorified. Right brain material is the stuff that dreams are made of and dreams will not get you status or wealth. We are taught that our metaphysical images have zero value - that there is only one reality and that science will ultimately master it.

Ironically, we get little or no encouragement for connecting with our Daimon from the Church. The Institutional Church generally discourages personal quests for the Divine. The Church provides us with creeds, dogma, and punitive consequences to discourage exploration of paths and byways off of the main highway.

Traditional churches present themselves as having at their disposal all the information one needs to have about spirituality. They purport that there is no need for a personal vision of god. They can tell you what he looks like (yes, in most cases, God is a male), how he thinks, and what he's going to do if you don't formulate a correct perception (their perception) of him. They promise salvation to card-carrying members and suggest that everyone else is in a heap of trouble.

Under the influence of these forces, the older I got the more I held my Daimon in disdain. I put him in my deepest internal closet and told him to stay there because he was childish, foolish and an embarrassment to me.

Having expunged all the magical notions that my Daimon from his position of interface with the gods had sent me, I proceeded to learn more and more facts. I learned so many facts that, by early adulthood, I figured I was getting close to knowing all there was to know. I had attained Twentieth Century enlightenment.

No two scenarios are identical. The dynamics of my split from my Daimon are undoubtedly different from yours in specifics but it's likely we have both gone through a separation.

Being a gift from God this spirit is not going to abandon us no matter how much we tell it to go away. All we can really do is put it out of our consciousness. When we do this, it becomes part of what

Carl Jung called the Shadow side of our personality. This means that, in consciousness, the Daimon is no longer recognized as part of us. It takes up residence in the Shadow which is the repository of all the aspects of ourselves which we choose to believe are "not me."

Chances are, being relegated to the Shadow has not prevented your Daimon from calling to you from time to time. We have all heard a still, small voice from within that speaks to us, more often than not in the quiet or in the night. This is the voice that sometimes warns us of impending danger, solves a problem that has us in a knot, or imparts to us some vital piece of wisdom. We call it intuition and, whether or not we give it heed, it is a reflection of the Daimon's powerful commitment to lead us.

What Good Is a Daimon, Anyway?

Many will say the exclusion of the Daimon from our conscious life costs us nothing. I agreed with this in years gone by. I thought science and her offspring, technology, would eventually provide us with explanations for everything and a quality of life that would be infinitely satisfying.

Though this expectation has not been met, I wish to make it clear that I am greatly appreciative of the artifacts of our scientific age. I do not romanticize the existence of pre-scientific people who struggled through life without the marvelous inventions and conveniences we know today.

It was not the fault of science but my naivete in assigning her a kind of omnipotence that led to my disappointment in her and a reconsideration of the value of my Daimon. It finally dawned on me that, in spite of ever growing scientific advancements, people were not getting any better. As a species we are a long way from being delivered from our discontent and our destructive ways.

I had failed to recognize that science too has her dark side that includes a ruthlessness and arrogance. She gave us a mechanistic universe that we felt free to tinker with and this allowed us to produce an abundance of material things designed to make our lives bigger, better, and easier.

Following scientific method enabled us to view the rocks, the plants, and the animals as mere objects for analysis and exploitation. They were completely despiritualized, no longer looked upon with reverence. The natural materials spawned by Mother Earth became our property to be used at whatever level of consumption it took to produce what we wanted.

When I first resumed listening to the small voice of my Daimon, he was saying, "Something is missing here." He still remembered what I had forgotten: that life is not simply a drama being played out around me; that I am an integral participant in that drama and am inseparably linked to all the rest of creation.

What the Daimon is good for, indispensable for, is his viewpoint. He shares the same sense of mystery and wonder that the earliest inhabitants of our planet knew. They recognized and showed reverence for the miracles going on all around them. They sought not to create miracles but to consciously participate in them.

This viewpoint, once adopted, will connect and keep you connected with the spiritual realm throughout each day of your life. Metaphorically, it conceptualizes life as a concert under the direction of an invisible maestro.

The Daimon does not seek the baton - he seeks the music. He knows that listening to the music will carry him ever closer to the orchestrator.

He joyfully participates in the same mysteries that have the effect of agitating our answer-demanding Ego. He accepts that there is a magical element woven into the fabric of all that is. He is serene in his awareness that everything that exists is in part unexplained and unexplainable.

Equally important to his viewpoint is the recognition that everything which exists is exerting some degree of influence, great or small, on everything else which exists. Exactly how and why this great concert of confluence continues to play is a mystery in itself. It is an ongoing magical process that has been in motion since the dawn of creation.

This constellation of influentially connected, created things is a Daimonic perception made conscious long ago by people who understood that the Earth, too, has a soul. Spurred by the contributions of Quantum Physics, the scientific world is now, at last, nervously beginning to explore this mystical connectedness of all things.

In spite of what our left brain may have to say about it, our sophisticated scientific explanations mostly lead us to more complex but nonetheless baffling questions. We are a long way from knowing it all and the Daimon says, "so be it." He would have us fully participate in the journey rather than place our emphasis on reaching a particular destination. The journey to which he beckons us, the quest for the Gleam, takes place just as much in inner space as it does in the external world.

An encounter with the Daimon confronts us with our ties to ancient history and fellow humans who are often called "primitive," but it does not demand throwing away your appliances or going to live in the wilderness. It hinges mostly on living your daily life from the vantage point of the Daimonic view.

This view involves accepting certain beliefs, attitudes, and behaviors that you may have been taught to reject. Although pockets of sub-culture may support them, our culture at large does not. This lack of cultural sanction is one of the circumstances that makes contacting and consciously utilizing the Daimon difficult. You find that the process not only arouses your own doubts and fears but also generates disapproval and criticism from others.

If these obstacles do not deter you, you are free to become increasingly aware of the Daimon beckoning you to explore the entire expanse of your psyche, mind, soul and spirit. This imaginative exploration will bring you in contact with unfamiliar landscapes and strange, even frightening, creatures. The Daimon, less fearful of such phenomena than the rational Ego, purposefully brings these things to your consciousness, knowing you cannot be whole until you cast a light onto the darkest corners of your inner being and integrate whatever you find there.

Be forewarned, then, that the task is scary and that most of the rewards it offers are subtle and deeply personal. Spirited imagination will not transport you to some over-the-rainbow utopia where troubles burst like lemon drops. The Daimon cannot take away the drudgery of life and an awareness of wonders does not eliminate hardship, pain, and sorrow.

Nor will everyone love and admire you for your expanded vision and increased wisdom. Remember that everyone else has, if they wish to pursue it, access to their own Daimon, so you will not be elevated to some superior status as a human being.

Ah, but there are some wonderful payoffs. Connecting with your Daimon will put you in touch with knowledge and healing powers that cannot be acquired through a rational, linear approach to life. Through your Daimon, you can enhance your mind/body system's natural ability to heal. You can explore your inner world at fantastic depths. You can increase your intuitive and creative abilities. You can establish more satisfying relationships with others. You can transcend the world of space, time, energy, and matter. You can actively seek a personal experience of the Divine.

You may experience a change in your ideas about who and what you are, about the nature of reality, about your relationship with the material universe, and about your spiritual connections. It's very exciting but it is also a leap into the unknown and we all have anxieties about that.

A Flurry of Wings in the Night

In the lives of some people, the Daimon for reasons not always clear will forcefully assert himself at a particular juncture. This happened to a client named Craig whose case will further develop our awareness of the burden and the glory of reconnecting.

Craig found himself in early retirement at age fifty-six. His executive position with a high-tech electronics firm had been high-teched out of existence.

This man who once flew missions as a helicopter pilot in Viet Nam, had loved corporate work and, though he was robust and enjoyed golf and tennis, he soon found he could not construct a rewarding life of retirement solely around these activities. His wife with whom he got along well had interests of her own and a heavy commitment to a community service organization. Their two children were grown and lived elsewhere.

Craig began to suffer from boredom and restlessness. He increased his alcohol intake and became critical of himself for not overcoming his inertia and getting more creative about his life. He was one year into his retirement in Florida when he scheduled a consultation with me.

At our first meeting, I observed that he was a handsome man, in good physical condition, with salt and pepper hair and dark, searching eyes. He outlined his problem, stating in summary that he needed "something more" out of life than he was getting.

He listened attentively as I noted that he was doing a lot of rational processing and that obviously it was not solving his problem. I suggested that he needed to find and utilize an inner resource other than his left brain and proposed that he get in touch with his Daimon for some direction toward how he could become more fulfilled in his new lifestyle.

He was interested in the concept of the Daimon and quickly reached an intellectual understanding of its roots but, when our discussion was done, he smiled, shook his head, and said politely that he couldn't see himself using the approach. He said he was too steeped in mathematics and circuitry to go off on trips of fantasy. He opted to continue to grope around for the present.

We left it that Craig could contact me if he changed his mind but my hunch was I would not see him again. I didn't realize that his visit had signaled the beginning of a siege by his awakened and energized Daimon. It came as a pleasant surprise when he called for a return appointment the following month.

At that second meeting, Craig said something peculiar had occurred about a week after his initial consultation. He awakened one night from what he assumed had been a nightmare. All he could remember about it was being alone in a valley with mountain walls on each side. Out of the darkness and silence there arose a sound like wings flapping.

The sound grew stronger with each passing moment and he became afraid because it sounded like a horde of birds or, perhaps, some strange unidentified beast. Just when the appearance of whatever it was seemed imminent, his eyes popped open. He was

41

aware of his heart pounding and the covers were damp from his perspiration.

The incident was alarming but he thought little of it afterward, mentally dismissing it as his stomach's protest over some Mexican food he had eaten prior to retiring. However, a few days later, the dream repeated itself and, although it was essentially the same, it was not so easy to rationalize away. Twice more it returned and Craig developed the notion that the dream image was for some unknown reason pursuing him, demanding to be confronted. After the third recurrence, he called for his appointment.

Craig, who had never paid much attention to his dreams, said rather sheepishly when we met again that the dream image had become clearer to him during the last recurrence. He had finally discerned the source of the disturbing sound.

It was being made by a monstrous bird with a wing span so great that it stirred the wind throughout the valley in which he stood. He could see the bird descending swiftly toward him with razor sharp talons outstretched. Once again, he awoke before it reached him and, once again, found himself in a state of anxiety.

Craig acknowledged that as he contemplated these dreams he came to the conclusion that they were related to our initial interview although he wasn't sure how. It struck him as ironic that, after declaring he could not engage in excursions into fantasy, he was suddenly overtaken by this vivid image which could not be dismissed.

I asked if he were willing to accept the possibility that the dream was a message from somewhere outside of his consciousness, inviting him to explore something about which he was unsure and anxious. He stated that under the circumstances it was a possibility he could not deny. He agreed he needed to explore the imagery further.

Following his assent, I instructed Craig in a relaxation procedure and suggested that he return in his imagination to the dark valley of his dream. In short order, he expressed having a sense of being there.

He described the valley as a dark and chilly place. The mountain walls on each side of him were high and steep. He felt utterly alone.

Somewhat reluctantly, he began listening for the sound that had frightened him. It came to him faintly at first, then amplified. It was so powerful that it reverberated off the mountain walls, making it difficult to determine which direction it was coming from.

The flurry of wings grew so powerful that it stirred the wind all around him, creating gale force gusts. He could see flashes of lighting of blinding intensity in every direction.

Finally, looking up, he observed the great, dark shadow of the bird approaching. He acknowledged being afraid and I could observe him moving his head and arms about in his chair.

I gave him verbal encouragement not to retreat from this creature, reminding him that, whatever its form, it was an image from his own Unconscious. I said it was some part of himself with which he needed to connect.

With sweaty palms and some twitching around his mouth, Craig held fast. He could see the giant creature descending rapidly toward him with talons spread. As it drew closer, he recognized it as a huge eagle, a creature he much admires. The steely talons plowed into the dirt just in front of him instead of into his face as he had feared and he became somewhat more relaxed.

After the landing, the scene became less dark. The bird was as big as the man was and, for a while, the two of them faced each other in silence. I requested that Craig thank the eagle for appearing and, after a few words of protest, he complied, saying the words out loud.

Then, I asked him to inquire about the eagle's name and he said, "This is all so far fetched." Nevertheless, he went on to ask and, to his surprise, the name came to him immediately. It was Sam.

With lessening resistance, Craig followed my suggestion to ask Sam why he had been pursuing him in his dreams. Part of the answer to that question came out in our present session and some of it unfolded as we continued to work with Sam over a period of time, but the image immediately identified himself as Craig's Guide (or Daimon). He stated he had been trying to force himself into Craig's consciousness for some time.

As the story unfolded, Sam informed us that, from the place in the Shadow where Craig had put him long ago, he had been energized by what transpired at Craig's first therapy session. It filtered down to Sam that I was proposing Craig should meet and work with him. Although the proposal was declined, Sam knew that a window had been left partially open and that it was his best chance to possibly reconnect with Craig.

That's when he started to intrude into Craig's dreams. He announced that he had been much more active in recent dreams than Craig realized, noting that the dreamer had forgotten several of his appearances upon awakening.

By taking the form of a dream image, Sam was graphically representing to Craig the problem that he most urgently needed to address. This was Craig's state of loneliness and isolation symbolized by the dark valley in which he found himself.

Knowing that Craig loved his piloting days, Sam's Daimon took the form of a creature of the air. He behaved in a frightening manner to insure getting Craig's attention. Had he been less threatening, he could have been more easily dismissed.

So it was that Craig and Sam met. Sam declared that his mission was to guide Craig in enriching his life and being all that he could be. In other words, he clearly defined himself as Craig's Daimon, an entity of which Craig knew nothing until our first therapy session.

Craig was incredulous but excited and continued to dialogue with Sam. Sam encouraged him to explore new activities. While investigating various possibilities, Craig made contact with a hot air balloonist and has since become an enthusiast. He says that when he goes aloft he feels like the Wizard of Oz.

Note the archetypal elements in Craig's original dream image. It begins in darkness, signaling that Craig has entered Shadow territory. The mountains are suggestive of the heights to which he aspires but which, because of his inertia, have become symbols of imprisonment.

Sam himself is an archetypal image. Native Americans associate the eagle with the power of the Great Spirit and in Greek mythology Zeus, the most powerful of the gods, was known to assume to form of an eagle.

Sam's arrival in the dream is preceded by wind, another symbol of the Spirit. It was the sound of the wind that heralded the arrival of the Holy Spirit on Pentecost in the Biblical story.

There was also lightning all about, similar to the tongues of fire in the same scriptural account. The lightning suggests that illumination or enlightenment is forthcoming.

The eagle comes as both messenger and guide. After conveying the message that there are yet undiscovered paths to travel, Sam proceeds to lead Craig to his new bliss: ballooning.

Craig's story exemplifies how persistent the Daimon can be but this is not always the case. Some Daimons seem to fall into despair and resign themselves to a continuing existence in the Shadow region.

We do not have to wait to be tracked down. We are all capable of reconnecting with our lost Daimon if we really want to. In the pages ahead we shall look at the specifics of how this is done.

CHAPTER FOUR

Learning To See The Ships

He thought he saw an Albatross
That fluttered round the lamp:
He looked again, and found it was
A Penny-Postage Stamp.

- Lewis Carroll
Sylvie and Bruno

In <u>Rhythms of Vision</u>, Lawrence Blair (1976) tells a story of the natives of Tierra del Fuego, an isolated culture, who navigated their waters by canoe. In the Sixteenth Century, when the Portuguese explorer, Magellan, brought his bulky sailing ships to their shores, these people were unable to see them. The vessels were so alien to their experience that the populace found it easier to regard them as invisible. The ships literally were beyond belief.

If we are to reconnect with our Daimon, we must learn to see the Daimonic equivalent of Magellan's ships. We must become more observant of things going on in our external environment and make new interpretations of our perceptions. We must open our eyes to the realm that lies beyond space, time, energy, and matter. As we do, we begin to get glimpses of the invisible ships that are anchored just beyond our conscious comprehension.

The Daimon's way of being aware accentuates the magic and mystery of both outer and inner existence. It grants equal credence to that which is immediately perceived and that which is not immediately perceivable. It takes into account the invisible forces which are implied in that which is observable, just as we all recognize the force represented by the unseen wind as it rustles the trees. "There is more," the Daimon says, "than meets the eye.

For the Daimon, life is unfolding on separate but interrelated planes. Occurrences in the realm of space, time, energy, and matter have impact on the nom-material realm of inner experience and vice-versa.

I should like to illustrate with a personal experience that is at once mundane and mystical.

An Encounter With A Hierophant

Years ago, when I was in the process of reconnecting with my Daimon, I had doubts about it making any real difference in my life and, therefore, was questioning whether it was worth the bother. In spite of my ambivalence, I had begun to notice an alteration in the way I was aware of internal and external events. I was experiencing a renewed sense of wonder in regard to life.

There was a brief but striking moment that brought home to me once and for all the special manner in which the Daimon perceives and interprets events. It occurred one ordinary morning at our ranch as I went about performing the never ending, menial tasks related to horse farming.

As I was pushing a wheelbarrow full of hay from one pasture to the next, a dark shadow passed over me. I immediately recognized it as belonging to a hawk. It was a commonplace event in the environs of our country home to which I would ordinarily pay scant attention.

My usual thinking process would have been to declare to myself that feeding time is a busy period and a hawk exhibiting normal hawk behavior does not justify attention.

On this particular morning, however, I found myself strangely unable to settle for this rationalization.

The familiar yet always impressive shadow of the hawk in flight awakened something unusual in me. I would not, could not it seemed, neatly classify the shadow's source in my mind and quickly dismiss it from my consciousness.

Though I did not know it at the time, my Daimon was asserting himself, probably energized by my recent efforts to connect with him. He compelled me to stop and raise my eyes to the source of the shadow.

Then, a remarkable thing happened. The red-tailed hawk screeched and swooped down to perch on a fence post only about eight feet from where I stood. This is unusually close inasmuch as I am sure he was aware of my presence.

I froze in my tracks and made a careful observation of my winged visitor. He, in turn, seemed to be observing me.

Suddenly, my vision became incredibly sharp. Every color in the hawk's plumage took on an uncanny richness and vibrancy. Every detail of his form was clearly delineated.

Though I cannot be sure of my accuracy, I intuitively identified my hawk as a male. His appearance and manner was that of a majestic overseer as he alternated his piercing gaze between me and the field before him, turning his head at right angles to his body.

As the bird and I shared these moments, it struck me that our encounter was no mere accident. There was something intentional about our having arrived together at that exact spot at that exact time.

The hawk and I were fully engaged with each other for a period of perhaps three minutes though it seemed more like ten. It was long enough for the bird to become much more to me than the caster of a fleeting shadow to be ignored. Thanks to my new, improved vision, I saw him as a messenger and a teacher.

Energy had passed between us. Some kind of mutual recognition had taken place. I do not hesitate to say that respect for each other was expressed.

At last, with a long backward glance toward me, the bird lunged forward and flew westward, the direction often associated with visions, dreams, quests, and journeys. I was flooded with my newly developing sense of wonder as I watched him disappear into the trees.

A message, which I believe the hawk delivered, burst into my consciousness. It said, "Follow me; follow the Gleam." He was pointing the way, encouraging me to resolve my doubt and ambivalence about the imaginal life.

The incident brought home to me the difference between my Daimon's awareness and that of my rational Ego. The Daimon was not interested in, maybe not capable of, classifying and dismissing the experience as the Ego would. He was unwilling to regard it as a random, meaningless event. He wanted me to stop and take the time to become a participant in the event. It was an encounter fraught with symbolism.

While the hawk was going about his business of being a raptor in the material world, for me he was also functioning as a hierophant, a revealer of sacred mysteries which I, in my effort to grow as a person, was trying to grasp.

His intense observation of his domain communicated to me more powerfully than the spoken or written word ever could a lesson I needed to learn. It told me in its visual language that I needed to keep my vision broad and to carefully observe the workings of nature.

In addition to this instruction, the hawk was announcing to me that my vision of life was about to expand and that my understanding of the sacred was about to change. Mircea Eliade (1964) used the term "hierophany" to describe this type of event.

Since the event transpired, I have had other hawk encounters. Each time I hear one's distinctive call and look up to see its spiraling flight in the blue dome of sky, I am reminded that I need to take the time to circle above the daily events of my life and to look at them from a higher perspective.

Years later, when I was working with my client Craig and Sam the eagle, as described in the previous chapter, I was struck by the similarity of the incidents awakening us to our Daimons, one occurring in the dream world and one in the material world. They serve to demonstrate how important information can be transmitted from spirit to Ego through events in both the internal and external worlds.

Seeing and Believing

Seeing and interpreting what we see is a process intrinsically bound up with our belief system. Any by-stander could easily have seen and made observations about my hawk's form and behavior. Undoubtedly, that person's account of what took place would differ from mine in many specifics or even gross aspects. As we move from a comparison of our perceptions onto our interpretations, the differences could be expected to increase markedly. At bottom line, we are left with the question: Who is right?

This question is one of the great spiritual pitfalls of Twenty-first Century Western Society. The left cerebral hemisphere of our brain likes the old adage, "seeing is believing" because it has a solid, grounded-in-fact ring to it. However, the other half of our brain might rather endorse the idea that "believing is seeing."

Those Tierra Del Fuego natives did not believe anything like Magellan's ships existed and could not perceive them. Similarly, the hometown folks in Nazareth who did not believe the carpenter's son had the power to promote healing did not observe any miracles when he visited.

Hypnotists have repeatedly demonstrated that, through the power of suggestion, a subject can be persuaded to see something that is not present in the environment, or to not see something, which is. Consider how much more influence our basic beliefs have on us over any hypnotic suggestion.

The fact is that, based on our experience and beliefs, we all see and don't see things differently. To understand why this is so, it is important that we recognize the incredible power of belief and focus on our personal belief systems which are to a great extent the creators of our personal world.

Each individual's belief system is bewilderingly complex. It is best described as a complicated, dynamic, psychosocial structure supporting certain acquired knowledge, ideals, and philosophical propositions. Our belief systems are heavily influenced by our surrounding culture and characterized on a personal level by intense emotional investment, vagueness, and inconsistencies.

Many people live out their lives without ever seriously examining their belief system. The process generates anxiety because it confronts us with difficulties that leave us confused and unsure. This discomfort is not surprising when you look at the following partial list of problems that must be faced.

1. Some beliefs are held consciously; some are unconscious. We like to think our outer behavior is congruent with our conscious beliefs and to a great extent it usually is. When we find ourselves reflecting certain attitudes and behaviors that go against our beliefs, it is probable that unconscious beliefs are being acted out. Are we willing to focus on and learn from such inconsistencies when they occur or do we brush them aside as some kind of insignificant anomaly?

2. Some of our consciously held beliefs are in direct conflict with others. By looking at which ones are given precedence and why, we can draw a conclusion about the relative strength of our various beliefs but this may mean having to face that there are some to which we only give lip service. Are we willing to confront this in our selves?

3. Some of our beliefs are supported and condoned by our surrounding environment while others are not. What do we do about those that are not? Do we bring them into the open, creating controversy, or hide them and preserve the peace? What determines our decision to do one or the other?

No wonder our mind is boggled when we attempt to sort out our beliefs!

Belief and Truth

In spite of this muddle, we draw from our belief system our ideas of what is true and not true. Since no two belief systems are exactly alike, we all have different ideas about what is true and what is possible. Between some individuals these differences are minimal and between others they are vast and alienating.

Human beings have considerable skill for interacting in spite of these differences but tend to hit a massive brick wall when it comes to those who purport to possess THE TRUTH. I am referring here to an absolute, not to be confused with the truth.

In Masks of the Universe, physicist Edward Harrison (1985) points out that, throughout the history of mankind, every age has subscribed to its own set of truths about the universe in which we live. Each set of truths in turn supported certain morals, manners, lifestyles, and bodies of knowledge. Each one prevailed until replaced by new, improved truths that won popular support and promoted change.

His point is that each of the many universes supported by its unique truths was the real universe for the people of its age but, obviously, each of them was only a mask of the universe. The real universe lies behind the accepted truths of the day. He proposes that our contemporary ideas of the universe and the truths which support them are no less a mask than those which have preceded them and will be replaced in time to come.

It is in this light that I respect my own views as my truth. I respect your views as your truth. I do not regard either set of views as THE TRUTH.

As far as I'm concerned, mankind does not know THE TRUTH at this stage of our evolution. From this philosophical position I can comfortably allow my Daimon to guide me on a daily journey to discover those truths which I need to confront in order to grow psychologically and spiritually.

In my encounters with clients and others I seek an exchange of truths. Sometimes I incorporate one of their truths into my belief system. I assume they do the same. It is not my goal to have them adopt my worldview.

When I present this perspective on the relativity of truth in public forums, the reaction of certain individuals and groups sometimes astounds me. It has called forth outrage from some Christians in particular, especially those who are committed to a literal interpretation of the Bible.

I have had that particular book waved at me with the pronouncement that it is the inerrant word of God. There are many that hold the entire package to be God's Absolute Truth revealed - THE TRUTH.

Logically, the argument quickly falls apart for me because the proof cited for THE TRUTH of the scriptures usually consists of quotations from the Bible itself, leaving the promoters in the not very strong position of arguing that the Bible is true because it says it is. Forgetting this and overlooking all the lies, factual distortions, and evidence of pious editing connected with both testaments, it is not difficult to see how this group identifies itself as the possessor of THE TRUTH.

The biblical text provides the kind of reinforcement which this or any group needs to maintain the notion that it is the possessor and keeper of THE TRUTH. For example some New Testament passages authoritatively declare that Christianity is the only path to a spiritual life beyond death. Often cited is John 14:6 wherein the author has

Jesus state, "I am the Way, the Truth and the Life. No one can come to the Father except through me."

That kind of cooks the goose for non-Christians. It is the gospel writer's intention, whether or not this is a saying actually spoken by Christ, to disempower all other belief systems and to pronounce Christianity the only valid approach to knowing God and attaining salvation.

Those who embrace this or other absolutes have no need for a spirit guide. Long ago, many Christian people were sold on the idea that one should rely solely on the Church and her teachings, not thinking for themselves. At this point, the Daimon became a dangerous and ultimately unwelcome ally redefined as the Demon.

The Daimonic view of the truth is supported by the history of our species and of religion which confirms that numerous truths of the past later have been declared erroneous by the institutional church and numerous errors of the past have been resurrected as truths. We have no cause to be so arrogant as to consider our modern ideas of truth to be inviolable.

It may be that the Universe and all it encompasses is less of a static thing and more of a giant process of change. If change is the very nature of all that is, then change can also be the nature of truth. Nothing remains the same.

Many people find these ideas frightening. Understandably, all of us who live in this uncertain world long for certainty. Unpredictability generates anxiety. If we possess THE TRUTH there is something permanent and unchanging for us to hang on to in the midst of the seeming chaos of evolutionary life.

The downside of THE TRUTH is that the certainty it brings into our lives can be maintained only by a strict avoidance of the truth. Once we possess THE TRUTH other perspectives may merit a degree of academic curiosity but they are essentially irrelevant and inapplicable in our lives. The only serious consideration given them is to point out their errors.

It becomes difficult to travel comfortably with those who do not share THE TRUTH. Those who believe it are by definition Right, while others are Wrong.

Those who do not ascribe to THE TRUTH become objects to be either converted or eliminated. Why should they receive tolerance for hanging around and doing things that bring into question the absolute, sacred knowledge that is sufficient and complete? How much importance should be attached to their having the opportunity to worship their false gods with their meaningless or perhaps odious rituals?

Elitism, persecution, and extermination are likely to become the behavioral ploys of the keepers of THE TRUTH, an observation well supported by history.

In contrast, a belief system regarded as the truth permits growth. There is room for additions and subtractions. It is not a closed system sealed with the sign of the Almighty. It allows us to learn from anyone, regardless of his or her orientation. It also places on each of us individual responsibility for identifying and rejecting potentially harmful and destructive teachings.

The person who identifies her belief system as the truth can allow it to be one system among others that are equally deserving of respect. This need not deter her from vigorously expounding on and defending her chosen beliefs but it is done in an open-minded spirit of tolerance. She may just as actively as anyone campaign for that set of beliefs which has expedited her growth and enriched her life on a personal level but she does not grandiosely assume that those beliefs will work just as well for everyone else and should become THE TRUTH for all. Many zealots and despots have mercilessly maimed and slaughtered in the name of promoting THE TRUTH.

A society which supports a diversity of institutions and belief systems is showing consideration for the uniqueness of each human personality. We're not all constructed to think, feel, or do things the same way. The rightness of the path is relative to the traveler.

If we do not accept this, it is difficult to see that the Daimon shows us a way that is true but only one of many roads to enlightenment. Professing that there are many paths to God, the Daimon follows Merlin's Gleam and appreciates all of the maps charting the course whether drawn by Lao Tzu, Buddha, Jesus, Mohammed, or the next door neighbor.

What is Possible and How Do We Know?

Our beliefs determine our concept of what can and can't be done, what is real and not real, who and what we are, and the meaning of life. Many of us prefer a belief system which allows for everything to be ultimately explainable and refutes the notion that there are forces at work within us and without which we may not recognize or, if we do, are beyond our understanding.

If this is our system of choice, there are only answers to be pursued, mysteries to be solved. The Daimon, on the other hand, beckons us to live the mystery and journey to the source, the metaphorical Gleam.

In his wonderful book, The Seven Mysteries of Life, Guy Murchie (1981) states the Daimon's perspective eloquently.

He calls attention to the otherworldly aspects of existence on our planet which, by most of us, go unnoticed in our daily lives. He cites such wonders as the way a bird's breakfast turns into a song and an acorn forgotten by a squirrel becomes a great oak in a hundred years. He espouses the Daimonic view of "something more." Most of us do not pay attention but, when we do, we can observe marvels happening all around us in our daily lives. Magellan's ships are waiting in the harbor to be seen.

I am inserting here as Exhibit A short list of phenomena that do not lend themselves to logical explanation. Some are based on personal observation but most have been cited in newspapers and on television broadcasts. I have used the latter sources with the presumption that they may lend a sense of familiarity and authenticity to the material but I encourage you to consider that such wonders are occurring every day in the universe and most are not publicly reported.

1. In 1965, a psychologist on the faculty of Columbia University heard the voice of an unseen entity instructing her to take notes on what it was about to dictate. Some seven years later a manuscript of 1500 pages had been recorded.

This collection of profound spiritual teachings became known to the world as A Course of Miracles (Foundation for Inner Peace, 1985). It was channeled through Dr. Helen Schuchman, an atheistic professor, whose colleague the equally non-spiritual William Thetford scribed her dictation.

Dr. Schuchman died in 1981 and controversy continues about the true source of this and other channeled works. Is the source of such works an outside entity communicating telepathically or a manifestation of some part of the self hidden in the Unconscious? No matter how you choose to interpret its origin, it is undeniably a remarkable piece of literature composed in a most extraordinary fashion.

2. Not long ago, a window of a commercial building in Florida developed hues and swirls that resulted in an image which many identified as the Virgin Mary. Thousands of visitors have come to the premises to observe the phenomenon and many have prayed there, lighting votive candles and leaving flowers. This particular apparition of the Virgin is unique in that it can be observed by just about everyone rather than one or a few individuals.

This is one of the most recent in a long and impressive history of visions of Mary, the most notable being her appearance to Bernadette at Lourdes in 1858 and her manifestation to three children at Fatima in 1917, accompanied by the famous solar apparition (the sun bounced and wheeled about the sky) attested to by thousands. The most celebrated recent vision occurred at Medjugorje and was reported by six children ranging in age from 10 to 17. All attested to seeing the Virgin holding the infant Jesus on a hill near their village. She identified herself as the Queen of Peace.

At Medjugorje the vision recurred almost daily over a period of several months. The children were given messages relating to penance, fasting, and prayer. The Virgin also promised that a visible sign would be given at some unspecified time in the future.

To say that this and other visions of the Virgin emanate from the imagination of those who report them may be a truth but is this an explanation? We must ask ourselves why this Archetypal Mother image recurs so frequently and inspires such a strong emotional response in so many people. What is it that generates this form in the imagination in the first place and what gives it so much power? One viewpoint, which Carl Jung might enthusiastically support, is that the goddess has been excluded so totally in Judaism and Christianity that the image of the Archetypal goddess (Mary) keeps intruding into our collective consciousness in an effort to establish a place for the Feminine Divine.

3. Another kind of image attracted a lot of attention in June 1991. A nine-year-old San Diego girl named Laura Arroyo disappeared from her home and, sixteen hours later, her body was found in the nearby town of Chula Vista. She had been murdered.

The following month, people in Chula Vista began reporting that little Laura's face was appearing on a blank billboard at the corner of Broadway and Main Street. The image, in the form of subtle shadows, appeared at night while floodlights illuminated the billboard. Soon, huge traffic jams were in place as thousands flocked to view the image. Large numbers of the viewers reported recognition of the child's face. This activity continued until the owners removed all lighting from the board.

An optical illusion? What is an optical illusion? Why did it resonate with little Laura's death? Why at this time? Why at this place?

4. My own experience, corroborated by other psychotherapists treating patients with Dissociative Identity Disorder (formerly known as Multiple Personality Disorder), has revealed that, at some point in therapy, there will probably emerge a special subself whose function is to help the afflicted individual integrate his or her several personalities. It is not unusual for this particular subself to refer to itself as a spirit or supernatural being and to exhibit astonishing healing power. Call it Daimon, Guardian Angel, Inner Healer, or what, it functions as an assistant to the therapist and sometimes gives excellent instruction to the therapist regarding how to proceed with the patient. It has the characteristics of an entity operating within the pathological system but not of it.

5. Clinical literature abounds with stories of cures brought about through unconventional means. One of the most compelling examples concerns a young boy suffering from a malignant brain tumor. Declared terminal, he was taken to the Mayo Clinic in Rochester, Minnesota, where a staff person suggested that he begin imaging his cancer and visualizing its destruction.

The child became intensely involved with images of rocket ships flying about in his head, firing their cannon at the tumor. After a few months of this, he declared his rocket ships could no longer locate the cancerous mass and requested a new x-ray of his head. His physician advised that the x-ray would be a waste of time and money.

Feeling better, the child returned to school and fell down on the playground. A CAT scan was ordered to assess possible injury and miraculously revealed, as the child had predicted, no trace of the once deadly tumor.

What process healed this child and how did he know he was healed before clinical verification took place? Medical specialists are inclined to call such events "spontaneous remissions." This labels them but does it explain them?

6. Janet, a client of mine, vividly recalls a car accident in which she was involved. It occurred when she was taking her two-year-old son to visit his grandmother who lived in the farming area. While rounding a curve on the rain slick country road, she lost control of the car. It slid into a ditch and turned over.

After a moment of being stunned, she roused herself and immediately noted that her baby, still strapped in his car seat, was unconscious. Unaware that the child was not seriously injured, Janet extricated herself from the vehicle with some difficulty and, retrieving her little boy, looked up and down the road. To her relief, she spotted a house about 100 yards away.

Janet ran with the baby to the house and pounded on the door. The elderly lady inside helped her with the child who was beginning to revive and called 911. Janet was puzzled when she heard the woman report <u>two</u> injured parties. Only then did she notice that her leg was swollen and bleeding. At the emergency room she was informed she had sustained a fracture, yet she had not been aware of the slightest pain while rushing her son to the house near the crash.

Of course, Janet's endorphins played a part but she told me that while she was running with the baby she felt as if her feet were not touching the ground. She felt lifted by some unseen force.

7. Early experiments designed to teach chimpanzees to speak words were strikingly unsuccessful because of the animals' insufficient anatomical structures for speech. However, following the

observation that chimps in the wild utilize a variety of communicative gestures, work on communicating with them through sign language has produced some impressive results.

The most astounding finding associated with such well known signing apes as Washoe, Koko, Lucy, and Sarah is that, once they acquired symbols representing various objects and behaviors, they spontaneously began to combine them into meaningful phrases. In doing so, these animals have progressed far beyond merely naming things and have demonstrated a grasp of the abstract concept or idea behind the sign.

Animal intelligence and more importantly animal wisdom has long been disdained by arrogant Homo Sapiens. Technology aside, might they know something more than we about life, love, pain, death, and the Divine? Animal guides often join the Daimon as she leads us on to the Gleam.

8. In 1953, a two year old Indian boy named Ravi Shankar began talking about having lived a prior life in a district neighboring his home. He described toys he had owned and knew the name and occupation (barber) of his previous father. To everyone's dismay, he also revealed that he had been murdered and quoted the murderer's name. He stated he had been eating guavas just before his assailant cut his throat.

Ravi's story spread about the country. When he was four, a man came to see the family stating his six-year-old son had died in the exact way Ravi described. The murder occurred six months before Ravi's birth.

American psychiatrist, Ian Stevenson, a researcher in the field of reincarnation, heard about the case and investigated it in 1964 when Ravi was thirteen years old. He discovered that Ravi's claims had been written down by a teacher when the boy was just five.

Using these notes, Stevenson was able to verify twenty-six statements the child had made, including the toys he possessed and the guava-eating incident. He also learned that the two families had a slight acquaintance but ruled out collusion inasmuch as Ravi's father had taken harsh steps to silence his son's talk about a past life, even beating him on one occasion.

The most remarkable feature of the case was young Ravi's phobia for knives and razors and his fear of going to the area where the other boy had been killed. To top it off, the youngster had a birthmark on his neck that closely resembled a scar that might have been left by a knife wound. The case is often cited as prime evidence of reincarnation.

9. Larry Dossey (1993) is a widely respected medical doctor who has gathered a lot of scientific data supporting the healing power of prayer. Many very respectable research designs have been employed to measure the impact of prayer on the process of surviving and recovering from surgery and illness, including protocols in which the patient did not know he or she was being prayed for.

Dossey cites experiments that demonstrate that prayer can have a positive effect on high blood pressure, asthma, headaches, anxiety, and cardiac problems. There is further evidence that positive results ensue not only when prayers are offered for specific results but also when they are offered for nothing specific at all.

People who are prayed for generally do better in recovering from a variety of medical problems but prayer is not a guarantee. Nevertheless, Dossey's serious studies seem to confirm what many have long believed: that prayer is a means of accessing the non-material universe.

10. On a television talk show in 1988, aerospace chemist Edward Butler revealed to the world a prophetic dream he had at age 25. At that time of his life he was employed at a plant where he worked with rocket engines and fuel.

Over a period of months, Butler had a recurring dream that depicted a violent explosion in the building where he worked. The dream scenario continued with his discovery, as he hurried out, of co-worker Rita Dudak with her body afire like a torch. It concluded with his dragging her to a safety shower and dousing the flames that engulfed her.

On April 23, 1959, Butler's dream became a reality in every detail. The phenomenon is called precognition but the label does not explain how this specific information was placed in Butler's consciousness.

11. July 4, 1826 marked the fiftieth anniversary of the signing of the Declaration of Independence and the first time that fireworks were used to celebrate the occasion. Incredibly, it is also the date when the two leading architects of the Declaration died. Thomas Jeferson and John Adams, living miles apart, gave up the ghost within hours of each other. Both had been suffering prolonged illness and those close to each man said they seemed to have willed themselves to survive to this date.

To what extent can we will ourselves to live or die? Can soul with the help of spirit arrange its departure time?

12. On a daily basis, a Labrador Retriever named Evangeline accompanies her owner, Catherine, everywhere she goes. Catherine suffers from a form of epilepsy that cannot be completely controlled with medication. She is subject with little warning to a grand mal seizure. It can occur at any time or any place and involves the possibility of serious injury from falling or colliding with objects in the environment.

Inexplicably, Evangeline is able to sense in advance the approach of Catherine's seizures. She signals her mistress by whining, jumping up, and licking her face profusely. When this behavior is observed, Catherine seeks out a quiet safe place to lie down before the convulsive episode begins.

Who or what is it that speaks to Evangeline of the approaching electrical storm in Catherine's brain? What is the spiritual connection between dog and mistress?

And what does this handful of stories suggest? They bring to my consciousness the image of my wife, Shirley, who died at age twenty-five of acute leukemia. Six months before her death while she appeared strong, healthy and free of any symptoms, I was awakened deep in the night by the sound of her crying into her pillow. I held her and asked what was wrong.

"I think I have a terrible disease and am going to die," she said. From what source did she get that information? Is there more going on than meets the eye? Are there sailing ships offshore?

Believing is seeing.

CHAPTER FIVE

The Stranger You Have Met Before

"Who are you?" said the Caterpillar.
This was not an encouraging opening for a conversation. Alice replied, rather shyly, "I - I hardly know, Sir, just at present - at least I know who I was when I got up this morning, but I think I must have been changed several times since then.

> - Lewis Carroll
> Alice's Adventures in Wonderland

What do you say when you meet a Daimon? How do you meet one in the first place?

If you've checked your belief system and find that it will allow for the existence of your Daimon, whom we have identified as your inner spiritual guide, you may wish to work on establishing conscious contact with it.

One of the first difficulties is recognizing it. Like all archetypes, the Daimon cannot be experienced directly. Therefore, we must content ourselves to interact with images representing it.

In Chapter Two we noted that Daimonic images are masked figures like the Lone Ranger. No matter how they represent themselves to us, there is always something more profound about them waiting to be unmasked. Some of their meaningful attributes may be immediately visible but most are not.

Given this characteristic, it behooves us to look more carefully at the form our images take, remembering that the image is a metaphor. I like to say that Daimonic images are adherents of the Lon Chaney tradition.

Chaney was a silent film star who appeared in well over one hundred roles from 1913 to 1930. He was known for his ability to play an astonishing variety of parts and, to this end, he was a master of makeup. So adept was he at this art that many filmgoers had no idea what the actor really looked like. To his fans he was known as the man of a thousand faces.

The Daimon, too, wears a thousand faces. Like many of Chaney's fans, we don't know what he really looks like. We only know the forms by which he manifests himself and these can be many. In ongoing contacts with your Daimon, expect his form to change. The changes may be subtle or drastic.

The cause of this diversity is to be found in us, not the Daimon archetype, which is an entity of constancy. Rather, it is we, who like Alice in Wonderland, are constantly undergoing change, not only year to year but hour to hour. Our alternating and shifting states of mind excite our imagination to create an image of the Daimon which emphasizes a particular trait or nuance of his essence today and another tomorrow.

Sometimes the Daimon's form may be altered in conjunction with a specialized task he is performing such as healing, problem solving, predicting, journeying, etc. but this is not a given. Some changes in form may have a deep symbolic meaning to be examined as part of the total message the Daimon is bringing you but neither is this written in stone.

Therefore, when we meet in consciousness, the Daimon often strikes us as a stranger who is eerily familiar. After all, he has dwelt within us since birth. In the process of coming to regard him as "not me" we have increasingly excluded him from our awareness and have lost touch with his shapeshifting ways. Upon reconnecting, we find we know him and don't know him at the same time.

Dramatically, the Daimonic manifestations are sometimes intrinsically linked to things or events in the material world and his message comes to us via something external to us. My hawk encounter is an example of this and the following story from my clinical files is an even more remarkable one. It concerns a client who, through unexpected events, had his long neglected Daimon brought into his consciousness by a creature in his environment. The experience was so profound that it caused him to question his sanity, seek psychotherapy, and ultimately to make some drastic changes in his life.

Norman G. Middleton, M.S.W.

The Dog That Woke The Farm Boy Up

Clint had grown up a country boy and knew the meaning of hard work. He and every member of his family had been assigned a proportionate share of the labor, which was required to keep his family's farm productive.

He described his father as a "hard man of the earth" who had practically no skills for self-expression. He demanded a lot from his four children and, until they were adolescents, meted out corporal punishment when they "did wrong." Yet, with much sacrifice, he laid enough money aside to allow each of them to have a college education.

Clint, the eldest child, stored up a mountain of resentment during childhood and adolescence. He liked living close to nature but felt oppressed by his work load and came to regard his parents as ignorant people (actually, they were just uneducated) doomed to toil and slave until their last breath. He did not want to share that fate and looked forward to going away to college as an escape from farm and family.

Though his academic performance was respectable, Clint quit his college program after two years. He decided that making money was his best assurance for never having to farm again and went to work for a contractor who had befriended him, learning all he could about every aspect of construction. He saw this as a way of enabling himself to start making bucks while his peers labored pennilessly on toward college graduation.

This decision turned out to be fortuitous. His employer recognized that he was alert, ambitious, and hard working. His earnings and responsibilities rapidly increased.

By his mid-thirties, Clint was a full partner in the firm. Along the way, he had married a young woman from a socially prominent family. He found her attractive but was not deeply in love with her. In time, he became aware that love was not her primary motivator for marriage either. Her relationship with Clint was her act of rebellion against her controlling parents.

Emotions notwithstanding, his bride's social status was important to Clint because it helped him to feel distant from his roots. He

64

retained a painful self-consciousness about having grown up in a poor, dirt-digging family.

The wife's name was Talia and their personalities were as different as their names suggest. They got along because he was willing to expend most of his time and energy on making money while she circulated at a couple of country clubs and maintained maximum involvement with her friends.

Though he didn't really enjoy them, Clint went willingly with Talia to "important" social events because they reassured him that he had truly risen from the cornfields. Because he was verbally gifted, he was able to project an aura of erudition as he rubbed elbows with the upper crust, hardly any of whom questioned his pedigree.

Truth be known, though, Clint never felt quite comfortable among the socially elite. Thursday nights were his to go out with some of the more affluent good old boys like himself. On these occasions his language was on the raunchy side and his drawl much more pronounced. He drank and played cards and had one hell of a good time. It was his favorite night of the week.

Talia was outraged when an unplanned pregnancy "happened." Conception took place when Clint came in drunk and horny after one of those nights out. She wanted an abortion but Clint wouldn't hear of it, so she went through with the birth and, as quickly as possible, turned the care of their little boy, Lyle, over to an expensive nanny with unimpeachable credentials.

Unlike his wife, Clint was enthralled with the child from the beginning. As the boy grew older, they spent more and more time together. To his surprise, the father found himself wanting his son to experience and enjoy the beauty of the land, the plants, and the animals. They closely bonded through such activities as shell collecting, fishing, and hiking in the woods.

When he turned five, Lyle began asking for a dog, setting off in Clint a wave of nostalgia over the dogs he grew up with on the farm. He regretfully remembered sometimes feeling that his father, who valued and respected all of his livestock, treated the four legged ones better than his children. In retrospect he realized his father loved animals and that he was endowed with the same feeling.

Clint went happily to the Humane Society to adopt a dog for Lyle. He found a robust puppy of mixed heritage whose outer appearance approximated that of a Golden Retriever. The dog displayed an affectionate nature and a high energy level that captured his heart. He was sure his son would like the pup but, regardless of that, he knew he had to have it for himself.

Talia's disdain for the new member of the family, christened Nugget, was unmistakable from the moment it was brought home. She successfully avoided contact with it most of the time. The only exception was on those occasions when Lyle would beg her to "give Nug a pat." Then, she would cringe and hold out a manicured hand that the irrepressibly affectionate dog would invariably lick, sending Talia off to the lavatory at quick step.

Her attitude mattered little to the males of the family. They and the dog were perfectly matched. They became an inseparable threesome.

This happiest of triads endured for just over a year. It was abruptly dissolved on a beautiful day in early summer when landscapers came to give the grounds a facelift. They left the front gate open and the ever-adventurous Nug, ready for action but totally lacking in street skills, escaped from the premises.

When his absence was discovered a frantic search was launched, bringing Clint home from the office. It was he who found their badly broken companion some two blocks from the house.

Nug lay nearly lifeless at the side of the road but managed a few wags of his tail as Clint approached. A wild ride to the vet's office ensued but was not quick enough. The patient was pronounced dead on arrival, the victim of a hit and run.

Father and son were grief stricken as they buried the cold inert remains of their once warm and energetic friend in a corner near the backyard fence where the otherwise abundant grass had always refused to grow. They discussed getting another dog right away but both decided they had to let Nug's memory fade before they could embrace a new pet.

Lyle moped and was tearful until the third day following the burial. When Clint came home that evening, the boy ran to him, excitedly claiming he had seen Nug's ghost during the afternoon. He happily reported that they had run and played together for several minutes and Nug had said he was quite content in "dog heaven."

Clint responded benignly, interpreting the experience as a fantasy created by his son to ease his grief. He thought no more about it until the weekend when, as he watched a baseball game on television, Lyle called to him frantically from outside to hurry out and see Nug.

Knowing there was nothing to see, Clint did not rush but he did join Lyle in the yard after a few minutes. The child's face was flushed and he was sweating under the summer sun.

"You should have come sooner, Dad," he said disappointedly. "Nug and I were playing chase. He ran off just before you got here."

"Oh," said Clint indulgently, "I'm sorry I missed him."

Lyle made a face reflecting displeasure. "Nug says you don't believe he comes here."

Clint put his arm around his son and walked him to a shady spot. "Well, I wish he did, Son. He's in my thoughts a lot just like he is in yours, but he's right. I don't believe in ghosts. You're seeing him in your imagination and that's o.k. because it helps you not to feel so bad. But there are no ghosts, dogs or human."

Lyle looked his father right in the eye. "Nug told me you'd say he's not real and he said not to worry about it. He said he'd fix you up with something you can see."

Clint smiled, patted his son's head, and there was no more talk about the dog between them for two full weeks. Then, while reading his Sunday paper, Clint was interrupted by cries of "Dad, Dad, come and look! Hurry!'

When he emerged into the back yard he found Lyle jumping around and pointing to Nug's gravesite. As the boy grabbed his hand and pulled him toward it, he could see a plant growing directly over the burial spot, the spot where not even a blade of grass had grown before.

Clint did not recognize the species but it looked to be some kind of wildflower. It bore small bright yellow buds that lent a cheery splash of color to that ordinarily somber corner of the premises.

Clint was incredulous. How in the world had the seed of that plant managed to anchor itself and grow rapidly in this one desolate spot on his well kept grounds? He asked Lyle if he had planted something there.

"No, sir," said the boy. "I think Nug made it grow."

At that instant, Clint was inexplicably shaken. He impulsively hugged his son and felt his eyes flood with tears.

After dinner the next day, Lyle approached his father and said, "Nug was here again this afternoon. I told him you liked the flower. He wagged his tail and went running off with a Dalmatian. I don't think he'll be coming back."

It turned out to be the boy's last report of seeing his beloved companion.

Over the next several days Clint could not shake the feeling that something portentous had taken place. He felt that a heretofore tightly closed part of his mind had opened up. He was deluged with memories of his childhood and discovered to his surprise that there were many pleasant ones intermingled with the bad ones on which he nearly always focused.

These thoughts and feelings culminated in a powerful urge to put his hands into the dirt. He wanted to make something grow. Most of his life he had wanted to get away from the dirt and now he was wanting to go back to it. He was completely baffled by his change of attitude and wondered if he was losing his grip on reality.

Clint presented all of this information to me in his mode of erudition rather than farm boy style. I listened attentively until he finished.

"What is it about these events that brings you to me, a psychotherapist?" I inquired as he looked at me expectantly.

"I'm not sure," he replied, shaking his head. "It's probably because I feel so irrational. I don't understand why I can't sort this out on my own."

He leaned forward in his chair, his hands clasped in front of him, and continued. "My dog got run over. My son imagined the dog came back to life and played with him. And a weed with yellow flowers grew on the dog's grave.

"This is all ordinary stuff. There's nothing about it that requires a supernatural explanation. Yet, I can't get over the feeling that it's some kind of lesson or miracle or something."

Clint sheepishly hung his head, appearing genuinely embarrassed.

"If it were a lesson, what would it be teaching you?" I asked.

My client showed signs of agitation, wringing his hands as he groped for an answer. "I don't know. I guess the lesson is that the facts don't fully explain what is going on."

"Is that something you need to have brought to your attention?" I waited as Clint spent a few moments in thoughtful silence.

Then, he began nodding his head. "Yeah," he said. "Yeah, I think it is. You know, I've lived my life in a very reactive way - always concentrating on avoiding or fixing what I didn't like about it. I don't know that I've ever given a thought to the idea of learning from experiences, especially bad ones, especially my childhood.

"As I told you, I've always been extremely negative about the way I was raised. I guess the truth is I feel sorry for myself because I was a farm kid with too many responsibilities and not enough praise.

"My self esteem was hurt because my parents didn't give me much spending money so I could buy nice clothes like other kids at school. When I was around them, I was always afraid they'd see some dirt on me from the fields. Whether they did or not, I know they looked down on me.

"The farthest I ever got with all this was a decision to, by God, leave it behind. That meant separating from my family as well. I only contact my parents a couple of times a year.

"I had no question about this being the right thing to do until this business with Nug. That stupid weed got me to thinking I want to grow things again. This, in turn, got me to thinking maybe there was something worthwhile about my childhood. I wonder if there is some meaning in it that I've missed."

"What could that be?" I wondered out loud, encouraging him to pursue his ideas further.

"Well..." He hesitated. "I don't feel comfortable taking about it but when I was in my teens I used to think my experience had prepared me for a kind of leadership. I had a sort of hero fantasy."

"What was that like?" I spoke softly in deference to his embarrassment.

"Well, you need to remember I was growing up when the threat of nuclear war was hanging over us all the time. I used to make up stories about the worst happening. I imagined desolation everywhere and pictured myself as this person who was important because I really knew how to survive. I knew the ways of the animals and how to live off the land. Because of this, I was appointed to be some kind of regional leader, taking my family and others into the wilderness and teaching them how to make a good life there. Everyone looked up to me."

"That's a great story," I declared. "You know, in mythology there are many wonderful tales about people being given sacred knowledge which empowers them in special ways. It's a theme that comes up again and again."

"Ah, well, it was totally stupid but, yeah, I guess that's exactly the kind of fantasy I had." Clint was smiling though I don't think he realized it.

"I don't agree about it being stupid," I countered, "because your fantasy was based on something very true about you. By virtue of that unsatisfactory childhood you mentioned, you became a Child of the Earth and wise in her ways. For that matter, you still are. You may have become a city dweller but you haven't lost that heritage."

As I talked, Clint became more animated. "I think that's what I'm realizing now. I tried to disown something that's a basic part of me. I may have left the farm and my family behind but I can't escape that part of myself. I don't think I really want to."

I could hear the call of the Daimon in what he was saying. It seemed like a good time to bring it more into his awareness.

"You went through a lot of pain and some hard times," I said, "but now you're sufficiently beyond that to listen to this part of you that knows there was also something wonderful in what you experienced. All that you learned and became during childhood contributes to your uniqueness as a human being. In spite of the pain that goes with it, it's a valuable part of you. Now that you are listening to it, it seems to be awakening you to the magical dimension of your developmental years."

Clint looked at me full face and I could see that his eyes were aglow. He no longer appeared embarrassed or confused. "So the lesson is that I should get back to my roots. My feeling that so strongly doesn't mean I'm losing it - it's more like I'm finding it. It just boggles my mind that this all got started by a dog and a little boy."

"I guess we could all learn a lot from dogs and little boys if we paid more attention," I observed.

"Man, this is getting mighty metaphysical," he declared, rubbing his cheeks with the palms of his hands like someone just waking up.

"Metaphysical?" I raised my eyebrows questioningly.

"Yeah." Clint nodded vigorously. "I've even been thinking Nug may have been sent to me by God or whoever runs things specifically to teach me the stuff we've been talking about."

"I can understand that thought," I responded. "When you look at what's happened one way, it's just a sequence of ordinary events. But, when you view it in the framework of things going on inside of you, it takes on inescapable significance. It's complicated to think about but it's like your inner world and the outer world are working in concert to bring something to your attention."

"Sign me on as a believer," Clint said. "I've been keeping this to myself but, as far as I'm concerned, there's a lot more at work here than just coincidence."

Clint's Daimon had been awakened by a hierophany. Whatever Nug's significance in the material universe, he was for this man a hierophant, a bringer of sacred truths.

It is accurate to say Clint's sleeping Daimon was aroused by forces operating without and within him - forces which seem to have been designed specifically to call the Daimon forth. The dog, especially in its ghostly form as perceived by Lyle, was instrumental in revealing to Clint the forgotten wonders of his difficult childhood.

Of course, none of this could have happened had it not been psychologically and spiritually the right moment for Clint to experience the awakening. At another time of his life he might not have noticed; he might not have cared. There is an adage that says when the student is ready to learn, the teacher appears.

Clint enlisted my help to learn more from his Daimon and we worked together for about six months. In imagery his Daimon took the form of a pig named VanBuren. Like Clint himself, VanBuren was a child of the dirt and grime. His aristocratic name was the name of a wealthy family Clint had known about when he was little. As

71

Clint followed VanBuren on a quest for the Gleam some enormous changes took place in his life, changes far beyond what is typical in psychospiritual therapy.

During our first two months of therapeutic work, Clint contacted his parents and paid them a visit during which reconciliation with them and his brothers took place. Thereafter, he and Lyle began making trips to the farm. Lyle took special delight in being close to his uncles and grandparents, the land, and the animals.

Clint's career was affected as well as he made some business contacts at his birthplace and began creating some innovative designs for farm buildings. These eventually drew the attention of a firm out of state that offered him a position to oversee the construction of his buildings in the southern region.

Clint was thrilled by the opportunity but Talia was distraught. Since it necessitated a move to a totally new area and a rural lifestyle, she saw it as a threat to her personal happiness. She declared that she would not under any circumstances relocate to "the boondocks."

Clint and Talia working out an amicable divorce agreement resolved the conflict. Clint was granted the status of primary parent to Lyle with a provision for unlimited visitation with his mother.

This story exemplifies one way in which someone may awaken almost unwillingly to their Daimon. It is more common to discover the Daimon by purposefully exploring inner images.

The story is also exceptional in terms of the dramatic circumstances surrounding Clint's awakening and the ultimate consequences. Many people connect and work with their Daimon without it causing such sweeping changes in their lives. However, it is not unusual for the process to bring about profound changes in one's perception of self, others, and the world. A person's attitudes, values, and beliefs are frequently affected.

If You Build It He Will Come

Though I've given you several examples of the Daimon in one way or another imposing herself on an individual, I hope it is clear to you that you do not have to wait for this. There are some not very difficult steps you can take to initiate contact.

In the 1989 motion picture <u>Field of Dreams</u>, an Iowa farmer hears a Daimonic voice urging him to build a baseball diamond on his property, suggesting that it will bring back from the dead the legendary baseball player, Shoeless Joe Jackson. The playing field is built and the magic works.

Fortunately you do not have to move earth or erect structures to meet your Daimon. However, the first step is to call upon your imagination to construct a meeting place.

If you build it, your Daimon will come.

Most of you have probably already created an imaginary field of dreams, a fantasy place that you like to visit - a place where you feel peaceful and at one with your surroundings. For one person this may be the seashore, for another a meadow, another deep woodlands, and still another a mountaintop. If you don't have such a scene already in place, it should not be difficult to create one.

The first step in Daimonic work calls upon you to use your imagination in this traditional way. The only preparation required is a comfortable setting and a block of time without interruption. Then, you spend a few minutes engaged in a brief relaxation procedure. If you have an already established method of relaxing, by all means use it. If not, make a recording of your voice reading the relaxation script in the Appendix of this book and play it back.

In your relaxed state, take yourself to that imagined setting where you know you would feel peaceful and at one with your surroundings. It may be modeled on some place you know or it may be pure invention. There are no fixed expectations. Just let this pleasing scene unfold before you.

When you arrive at your special place spend some time just being there. Let it become your reality of the moment. Pay attention to everything around you - not just sights, but sounds, smells, tastes, temperature. Note every sensation. This process locks your focus inward and energizes your imagination.

After you've explored this place, make yourself comfortable there and, once again, open up your consciousness. It is at this point that you are called upon to engage your imagination in a manner that departs from the daydream model.

We all know how to daydream and create specific images but it is important that you do something different for this experience. This time you are not to direct or instruct your imagination. You are to request something from it and wait for a response. This is the only "rule" for spirited imagining and it is essential.

Having placed yourself in your favorite imaginary surroundings, you are to ask your Unconscious to send you an image representing your Daimon. That's all. Just make the request one time and wait patiently.

It is important that you make no conscious effort to create an image. The idea is simply to allow one to appear. You need only to remain alert to whatever enters your awareness and to be accepting of any image that appears no matter how outlandish it may seem to you. Remember that the Daimon can and does assume a wide variety of forms, so be prepared to accept whatever emerges, be it human, animal, vegetable, mineral, or abstract.

Usually an image will present itself within a few minutes. It is reasonable to wait for ten to fifteen minutes if nothing appears sooner but not if you find yourself getting tense or anxious. If nothing presents on the first try, it is very likely you will have success on the second or third. There is also the possibility that a Daimonic image will come to you in a dream after you have bidden its presence. Pay close attention to your dreams during the night following this procedure.

If you think the image that arises has absolutely no relevance to the entity we call the Daimon, you should still hold on to it and work with it. Trust your Unconscious to know more about what is representative of the Daimon than you.

When your image comes into focus treat it with respect. Talk to it as if it were a material presence. Thank it for coming to you. Ask it if it is, indeed, your Daimon and listen for a response. The response will probably come to you as an auditory or telepathic message. It may take a little time. Don't rush.

If you get a negative response, ask this image if it can help you get in touch with your Daimon. There is a good chance that it was sent to do exactly that.

If you get a positive response, enter into an active dialogue with your Daimon. Tell it that you invited it into your consciousness because you want to learn from it and benefit from its power. (Declare this only if you really mean it.)

Ask some questions. Find out if your Daimon has a name. Ask it how it has been in touch with you in the past.

Ask it how it is willing to help you. Ask what you must do in return for the help.

Don't try to do too much at the first meeting. Schedule a time for your next meeting and say good-bye for the time being.

Once the Daimon has departed, slowly return to ordinary consciousness and open your eyes. Spend some time reflecting on what you feel, how you responded to your visiting image, and how it responded to you. You might wish to record these observations in a notebook that will become the journal of your travels with the Daimon.

You have met the stranger you have met before. The quest for the Gleam has begun.

CHAPTER SIX

If You Don't Scare Yourself, Someone Else Will

Though I'm fearful of the cellars where beasts of darkness hide,
I will climb into their depths if you'll linger at my side.

> \- Norman Middleton
> The Caverns of My Mind

Now that you are in touch with some kind of image that represents your Daimon, you can begin to interact with it in a variety of ways. The most difficult part of the interaction is allowing the Daimon to lead you. It is essential that you do not let your Ego dictate the imagery.

It is at this juncture that many people break out in a bit of a sweat. For most of us, giving up control over our imagination is a scary act. We've all heard disturbing stories about people who let their imagination "run wild." It comes close to our idea of what it means to be crazy.

Do we want to allow this entity to guide us? Where might it take us? To insanity? To depravity? To the Evil One?

Remember that the Greeks believed we have the power to use our Daimon for good or ill, though it was given to us as a protector and spiritual guide. If we will it to reveal, energize, and help us to exploit the evil in ourselves and others, this can no doubt be accomplished. It is a loathsome perversion of the quest for the Gleam.

In the spirit world there are evil entities as well as good. In our pursuit of light (the Gleam) we must traverse the darkness. Our archetypal heritage includes entities that would destroy the good and revel in violence, debauchery, domination, greed, exploitation, and other abuses. These demonic forms reside within us, mostly on the Shadow side, but must be encountered and integrated when they arise to block our spiritual path. Like all of the mythic heroes who have made the mythic journey, we will be tested and tempted. The Daimon will help us to stay the course.

If you have been long out of touch with your Daimon it may be difficult for you to have faith in it. Hopefully that faith will increase as we proceed through the pages ahead.

The early stages of reconnection may be like a honeymoon period. As you spend more time with your Daimon, you become aware of changes in your observations and your interpretations of what you perceive to be happening in the external environment and your own psyche. Your imaginative and creative abilities are energized. An ordinary trip to the park becomes an excursion into a magical realm. You feel a call to be with others who are spiritual pilgrims.

At some point your Daimon will beckon you to journey to places which are farther abroad from daily life and much less familiar. You will be led into the dark deep caverns of your mind - into the abyss, the endless night, the lair of the dragon, the inferno. This is what makes traveling with the Daimon a heroic journey, the kind of journey chronicled by all the great spiritual figures of mythology.

What To Do When the Devil Arrives

I was privileged to accompany a client named Corin on her spiritual quest several years ago. She had far more fear about imagery work than the average person. She was a pretty, dark haired woman in her late twenties who came to therapy because she was experiencing her marriage of three years as dull, passionless, and lacking in spontaneity.

She verbalized these complaints hesitantly because she had a strong religious orientation and the relationship seemed to meet the criteria of a Christ-centered marriage according to her religious denomination. She feared she was being selfish in wanting the marriage to be anything more.

Corin's husband was a fervent fundamentalist and a youth group leader in their church. This is where she met him after being "used" (sexually) and dumped in two prior relationships. She saw in his religiosity a sign of purity, strong moral character, and a commitment to follow in the footsteps of the Lord. To her, he appeared to be safe.

After their wedding she discovered that she had gotten exactly what she saw. Ben was sincerely though rigidly religious. When people spoke of him they usually commented on what a "good man" he was.

Ben was a virgin when they married and, unfortunately, sexually inept. When his disappointed bride tried to discuss this problem with him, he acted shocked and accused her of wanting to do "perverted" things. He defended his inhibitions with quotes from scripture. Ultimately, Corin felt ashamed about her sexual desires and stopped talking about them.

Both of these young people worked and their life outside of their jobs was structured entirely around church activities. They attended services on Wednesday evenings and twice on Sunday. Almost every week there were meetings of one or another parish organization to be attended as well.

Otherwise, they ate out about twice a month. Ben would have no part of movies, dancing, or any activity taking place where alcohol was being served.

On the plus side, Ben seldom raised his voice. He treated Corin and everyone else kindly. Only a couple of her more liberated girlfriends sympathized with her dissatisfaction.

After describing her circumstances Corin looked pleadingly at me and said she felt extremely confused. She had thought of discussing the problem with her pastor but had heard him say frequently that Ben was one of the finest Christian young men he had ever known. Though it felt risky, she decided to seek out a secular counselor, closed her eyes and pointed a finger at the telephone yellow pages. My name came up.

When I asked what she would like to get out of counseling, she said she wanted help in deciding what, if anything, she should, could, or would do to change her situation. I recognized that, for her, this was very much a spiritual issue and suggested that connecting with her personal spiritual guide would be the place to start. We spent the remainder of the session discussing the function of the Daimon and she responded positively to the concept.

At our next session, the client's Daimon appeared in the form of a cute little mouse named Brigit. Corin loved the image and asked

Brigit if she could help her get on the right path toward fulfillment of her destiny.

Brigit immediately told Corin to follow and, after taking her through what seemed to be a dark tunnel, arrived with her at a castle situated on the side of a cliff jutting up from the sea. It reminded Corin of the setting of some of the gothic romance novels she had loved to read on the sly in her teen years.

The scene was hazy at first but gradually cleared. As it did, Corin was able to discern the figure of a woman who looked much like herself standing outside of the castle. She was barefoot and clad in a diaphanous white garment. A rather strong wind was blowing her hair and clothes, as she stood motionless.

Corin was surprised to find she could read this woman's mind. She discovered that the woman knew there was a handsome, lonely prince waiting for her within the castle walls. The woman stood as if paralyzed because, although a part of her was feeling an urge to run across the wooden ramp bridging the moat, another part was overcome with fear.

The fear won out. The woman stood still, listening to the crashing of the waves below and made no advance toward the castle.

During this hesitant period Corin asked the image her name and she replied, "Helen." When asked if she were going to enter the castle, she said, "maybe" but after standing a few moments more she said, "no, I'm married, you know."

Feeling sad for Helen in her ambivalence, Corin asked Brigit to bring her back to her chair in my office. A short time later, she bade Brigit good-bye until their next meeting and returned to ordinary consciousness.

I encouraged her to allow her left brain to analyze and evaluate the imagery experience. She immediately realized that Brigit had helped her by projecting her problem onto Helen. It allowed her to look at it from the position of an observer, diminishing her anxiety, but she knew she and Helen were one.

Helen's dilemma was the same as Corin's. She really wanted a sexual encounter with an exciting, powerful male (a prince no less) but was too fearful to act on her desire.

When I asked her about the name "Helen," she said she didn't know any Helens but she associated the name with Helen of Troy about whom she knew little except for the fact that she was somehow the cause of a terrible war in ancient times.

I clarified for her that, according to legend, Helen was a beautiful, sensuous, and respectably married Greek woman who was abducted by the Trojan prince, Paris, inciting an aggressive response on the part of the Greeks as recounted in Homer's (1965), The Iliad. With further discussion, Corin began to draw parallels between her Helen, who is a representation of her sensuality and sexuality, and the Helen of Homer's epic.

Corin resonated with Helen of Troy's initial standing as the proper wife of a good man. His name was Menelaus, King of Sparta.

Being attractive and alluring led to Helen being chosen by the goddess Aphrodite to become the wife of her favorite, Prince Paris. Wishing to bestow on him the most beautiful woman in the world, the goddess helped him abduct Helen, whereupon he made her his consort and kept her confined within the walls of Troy for nineteen years. After the war, Menelaus took Helen back to Sparta where she presided once again over his royal palace.

Corin's fear was that she might be letting her sexual needs "take her away" from her home and marriage. Would she end up a prisoner of those needs? Would she be setting off a war between the conflicting sides of her psyche? Would some kind of destructiveness result from that? Would some alien gods or even devils take over her being?

At her next imagery session Corin asked Brigit how she should proceed and Brigit advised her to get to know Helen better. With that, she was transported to the previous scene and found everything just as before.

There was one difference. This time, Helen was moving toward the castle. With each step she seemed to be gaining confidence. Showing some signs of trepidation, she persevered and, at last, planted her feet on the drawbridge. Slowly, she began to walk across it.

At mid-point, she stopped in horror. Corin could see what Helen saw and shuddered.

They observed two dwarfish devils guarding the entrance to the castle. They had tails and horns protruding from the greasy, matted hair at the top of their heads. They were naked and it was impossible to ignore their genitals. Their penises were thick and gnarled. Their skin was mottled red.

The devils were grinning lecherously at Helen and waving for her to come on across. They called her a "cunt" and a "whore" and promised her a "good fucking."

Helen screamed and turned to flee. At the same moment, my client's eyes popped open. She had been propelled back to ordinary consciousness. She was pale and breathing hard.

"Demons!" she muttered, rolling her head about. "Unholy demons. Oh, my God!"

"Yes, demons," I said soothingly, "but be aware that they don't come from some external source of Evil. They are images projected by your own Unconscious. They represent your own conviction that your desire to be romantically and sexually fulfilled is dirty and bad."

We discussed the symbolism of her imaged devils at length. They were fitting representations of the depravity that Corin feared was behind her desire to "find the prince." They were present to frighten and deter her from pursuing that course and they succeeded completely. By finding herself scared out of her wits by these projections, the case against having anything more to do with Helen or the imagery process was made.

It took some intense therapeutic effort to help Corin return to an appreciation of the fact that it was Brigit, her Daimon, who brought her to Helen, the castle, and the devils in response to her request that she be shown the right path to fulfillment. Obviously, Brigit thought there was something important to be learned there.

The Daimonic principle allows for our demons to be teachers. The Daimon makes no effort to avoid and, in many cases, confronts us with them. She knows we must eventually integrate them if we are to grow in wholeness. It may also be her way of testing whether we have the courage and determination to journey with her.

I have a crude saying that I impart to all of my clients who are engaged in spiritual travels. It totally captures the essence of what we are discussing here. I say, "The only way you can slay a dragon is by looking it up the ass-hole."

There are aspects of ourselves which all of us want to avoid like the plague. These are the parts that we perceive to be so immoral, unacceptable, deranged, abominable, dangerous, and hideous that, if we allow them into consciousness at all, we would rather walk through the fires of hell than acknowledge them. Denying them and fleeing from them only succeeds in allowing them to have a life of their own outside of our awareness.

These are our personal dragons. Not only must we face and subdue them, but also we must face the most disgusting aspects of them.

As Corin began to understand the importance of returning to confront her devils and gathered her courage, there were others in her life who did their best to fan her fears. Most of these were friends and confidantes (all members of her church) with whom she discussed her imagery. Though some stated the message more emphatically than others did, the consensus was that she should not only stop imaging but should also stop therapy. One person told her she was gambling with her soul. As if she hadn't already scared herself enough, she was getting some help from others.

The Dragon Viewed From the Rear

Amazingly, Corin decided to return once again to Helen and to support her in her effort to find the prince. Guided once again by Brigit, she returned, found Helen, and offered to walk by her side to the gate of the castle. When they reached the drawbridge the little devils became visible as before but this time Corin called out to them.

"My name is Corin," she declared, "and this is my friend, Helen. You can just shut your dirty mouths because Helen is no whore. She's a woman with a healthy interest in sex who needs to explore her options. We're going to do that together by going inside the castle and you're not going to stop us."

The demons fell quiet, surprisingly subdued, as the two women approached them. On closer inspection, Corin recognized them as exact copies of some line drawings she had seen years ago in a book about the tortures of hell. She made a special effort to observe their penises and took pleasure in noting that in spite of all their bravado the little organs remained flaccid. They were not the highly sexualized little creatures she had thought them to be. It occurred to her that they were impotent.

Later, she would draw from this observation the lesson that she was in no real danger of being possessed by some supernatural being who would lead her into a wanton lifestyle. The real problem was what to do about her normal desire for a flesh and blood sexual partner.

As Helen and Corin walked past the devils, the huge doors of the castle swung wide, admitting them. The interior of the building proved disappointing. It was spacious enough but far from elegant. It was cold and austere with meager furnishings. They immediately made their way to the bedroom where they found the prince lying on his billowy bed.

He was a handsome young man but was languidly reserved as he waved a hand, motioning for them to come in. Corin was annoyed that he expected them to come to him rather than rising to greet them. After they entered the room, Helen took several steps toward the bed, then stopped.

"Why," she asked, "did you allow those demons to block my way to you?" Her tone was angry. Corin beamed approval.

"They are very fierce creatures," he replied in a soft voice. "I don't want to do battle with them. They might hurt me."

Helen glared. "And if they hurt me?"

"The risk is yours to take or not," he stated matter-of-factly.

"And what do you have to offer me now that I'm here?" she continued in a demanding tone of voice.

The prince raised himself on one arm and looked at her. "Myself, of course. I am here to give you pleasure at any time in any way you wish."

There was a pause before Helen spoke again. "I can see why you are all alone here in this cold place," she said.

She then turned to Corin. "I am not so desperate as to settle for this. This man is attractive but one-dimensional. He's like a machine that dispenses sex with no warmth or love. I want a man to satisfy me but I want him to be a lover."

Helen took Corin by the arm and together they made their way outside where they continued their dialogue. They concurred that the castle had no soul and was no place to dwell.

At that point, Corin told Helen that her home had plenty of soul but lacked sensuality. Helen offered to help her bring that dimension into the home. She volunteered to be supportively present if Corin would once again seek to motivate Ben to discover his sexuality. The offer was gratefully accepted by Helen who acknowledged that, when Ben had expressed shock regarding her sexual preferences, she had meekly backed off, concluding that she was indeed seeking something bad.

So it was that, by allowing Brigit to lead her, Corin and her sensual sub-self, Helen, became integrated, each drawing new strength from the other in order to overcome fears and to take a creative approach to problem solving. It now seemed quite clear to her that her husband had a pathological fear of his own sexuality, which, in turn, led him to reject hers.

Following their mutually agreed upon plan, Corin implored Ben to spend an evening at home with her to discuss "something important." When the moment arrived she could strongly feel the inner presence of Helen.

She told Ben the entire story of her meeting with Helen and their visit to the castle. Thanks to Helen's support, her words flowed with calm assurance. To her surprise, her husband listened attentively.

At the end of the narrative, she explained to Ben that she deeply valued Helen as a vital part of her personality. She expressed the conviction that Helen represents healthy sexuality, not wantonness. She told Ben she needed his help to keep Helen alive because, if Helen did not thrive, she would be subject to depression and resentment.

Their dialogue continued for a couple of hours and culminated in their agreeing to consult a sex therapist. Follow-up visits with Corin revealed that Ben initially had a tough time in therapy but finally started to "get it." The turning point came when he informed their pastor that their marriage was in need of priority attention and that they would have to cut back on some of their church related activities.

At last report, Corin was still consulting with Brigit.

The Dark Side of the Daimon

Corin's fears about Daimonic work were mostly generated as a psychological defense mechanism designed to control a part of herself which she perceived as very powerful and very dangerous. Apart from such defensiveness, however, a dark side of the Daimon can be recognized. It is this dark side which enables some individuals to generate destructive energy from it, thus materializing the Demonic form so feared and reviled in Judeo/Christian tradition.

In many societies, an individual's cultivation of the Daimonic dark side has been interpreted as an invasion by an evil spirit. There has been a degree of comfort in this concept because it maintains that the host is not an evil person, just one whose body/mind has been invaded by an external force.

The historical downside of this viewpoint is that those not similarly affected have felt obliged to use all sorts of horrendous tortures to convince the bad spirit to depart from the body of the possessed. The perennial downside is that it enables some individuals to deny responsibility for their wrongdoing.

Of course, it has also been maintained that good spirits take possession of us too, leading to the question of just who the hell we are without one or the other of these entities in charge of us. The widely held belief in the Holy Spirit of Christendom is an example of good spirit possession. According to doctrine, the Holy Spirit is not inborn but is conferred on us at Baptism and remains with us thereafter throughout life, carrying out Daimonic functions.

For centuries, people have derived great comfort from the notion of good spiritual beings helping and supporting them on their life journey. Both Judaism and Christianity support the belief in separately created beings called angels, especially guardian angels, who also have Daimonic qualities.

With all of this good help available, it is not surprising that the concept of equally powerful and intrusive devils became a primary explanation for evil. It became generally accepted that a great battle between good and evil, God and the Devil, angels and demons, was constantly being fought in the external world and that mere mortals were frequently being used as pawns in that contest.

While the concept of the Daimon is obscure to most people today, demons (defined as evil spirits) remain familiar to just about everyone. In fact, the Daimon and the evil demon are two very different entities. The demon is by definition purely evil and unredeemable.

The Daimon's attributes are predominately positive, creative, protective, and life enhancing. The Daimon is an intimate, inner structure with which we are endowed from our beginning. It does not overpower us. Rather it is we who use the Daimon and can if we choose use it for ill purposes.

What, then, is the dark side of the Daimon and what kind of self-defeating behaviors are associated with it?

The Ego, the executive part of our personality, prospers by being in touch with the Daimon and allowing him/her to lead the way toward the Gleam. This connection becomes distorted and destructive when the Ego identifies itself as the Daimon. Jungians call this identifying with the archetype.

When this occurs, one's recognition of the Daimon's place among one's subselves is lost and energy is obsessively invested in actually presenting one's self as this supernatural being. Those who do this almost always go public in order to feed their pathologically expanded, unbounded Egos. Examples may be found in the exploits of the now famous televangelists, many political figures, and some self-proclaimed spiritual adepts.

A more subtle display of this same problem can be observed in situations where someone infuses her profession or occupation with Daimonic overtones. What emerges is the Daimon masked and costumed as the doctor, lawyer, engineer, artist, athlete, teacher, architect, etc. Regardless of her skills in a given field, which may be considerable, we are struck by this person's arrogance and grandiosity.

Others who are out of balance may actively seek to develop and identify with the Daimonic dark side for the purpose of becoming the

Demon. Someone who feels too inadequate and inferior to strive for positive recognition may decide to present himself as possessing all the power that goes with badness. This person may concentrate on ways of using natural magic exploitatively, even to the point of deceiving or inflicting harm on others.

History supports the observation that the creative power of the Daimon can also be misused. Think of all the genius and creative effort that has gone into the design and manufacture of weapons of mass destruction. Ponder the clever planning behind the execution of sophisticated crimes at all levels of society. Take note of the considerable talent that is perverted by creators of art forms that appeal to the basest and sickest interests of the public. Recall the fate of followers of charismatic leaders like Jim Jones who were led to acts of suicide and murder deep in the jungles of Guyana.

Investment in the dark side of the Daimon can lead to self-defeat and/or tragedy. On the Daimonic journey, the rational Ego must maintain its function even as it must allow itself to be led. The journey is a team effort, a balancing act.

Where Can You Take Your Daimon On A Date?

Once you've calmed your own fears about dating your Daimon, where can you go in public with him? You can go anywhere, of course, but it pays to be sensitive to the tremendous amount of fear and hostility regarding Daimonic work that is extant in our society.

Corin, whom you met earlier in this chapter, found that her Daimon was not welcome at her church and many others have made the same discovery. Seeking transcendent experience with your Daimon as your guide is not going to be an activity endorsed by most religious institutions. The process is too idiosyncratic. What you discover may not be compatible with the creeds or the denominational interpretation of scripture. Some of my Christian clients have substituted terminology when talking with church folk, referring to the Daimon as their guardian angel. Even this does not fly well, however, when they allude to using their imagination to connect with the spiritual realm.

So, if you take your Daimon to church be prepared to be labeled a maverick or worse. If it's any consolation, keep in mind that this is the same label that the church attached to some of its most famous sons and daughters such as Thomas Aquinas, Joan of Arc, John of the Cross, Teresa of Avila, and others. They all had run-ins with the ecclesiastical authorities.

It is not my intention to single out the Church. North American society as a whole is not receptive to a psychospiritual approach to life. As a case in point, think back to June 1996 when Hillary Clinton came under extensive media criticism.

Mrs. Clinton had been consulting with Jean Houston, a widely respected psychologist noted for her therapeutic use of guided imagery. In the course of their working together, Houston apparently encouraged the First Lady to dialogue with an image of Eleanor Roosevelt, whom she much admired. When news of this event was leaked to the press it was maligned as a seance and it was explicitly suggested that Hillary is an occultist.

My conclusion is that many North Americans have not come very far from the days of the Salem witch-hunts. God forbid that anyone should break out of the fold and follow a spiritual path that has not been granted an imprimatur.

Despite the lack of sanction many people are doing just that. Many of us are aware that there is a tremendous restlessness abroad, a longing to pursue the Gleam without fetters. Individuals are turning to all kinds of new approaches to accomplish what established social institutions have failed to do. As with most breakaway operations, their course is veering, sometimes taking them beyond the borders of reason, but this does not negate the legitimate purpose of their sojourn.

If you want to go public with your Daimon, while you may hit some barriers with the established social order, remember there are other pilgrims out there. You can test the water by sharing some of your experience with others with whom you have already built trust. It doesn't take long to get the drift of most people's attitude.

Contact with fellow travelers can enrich the psychospiritual experience but it is not essential. After all, the world of imagination is both private and complete and there are already within you alone others who are ready to embark.

CHAPTER SEVEN

The Jabberwocky Issue

"It seems very pretty," she said when she had finished it, "but it's rather hard to understand." (You see she didn't like to confess, even to herself, that she couldn't make it out at all.) "Somehow it seems to fill my head with ideas - only I don't exactly know what they are!..."

> - Lewis Carroll
> Through the Looking-Glass

Once we are reconnected to our Daimon, we may find communication with her difficult. Unaccustomed as we are to extensively employing metaphor and symbolism in our lexical activities, we may initially feel the need for a translator. Like Alice upon exposure to Jabberwocky, we may feel that the Daimon has transmitted something meaningful but be unsure about exactly what that meaning is.

In previous chapters we noted that the Daimon's predominant language is imagery. It is a mode of communication that is very different from the verbal, where the words utilized have a more or less precise definition. We can always look them up in the dictionary.

Images, before they are translated into words, are much more dynamic. They tend to slip in and out of our consciousness with more fluidity than words and, even when they are retained in consciousness, their presentation is shimmering, their form subject to change from moment to moment, and their attributes in constant flux.

Spirited images are by nature metaphorical. They are our encounters with the unknown, unseen. Our imagination is stimulated to give these mysteries form and may use familiar or unfamiliar persons, animals, plants, objects, places, and events to give them that form. The beauty of it all is that the selected metaphor will have deep and genuine meaning to the imaginer, though this may not be immediately comprehended. The metaphor will be just right, based on that person's experience and needs.

For this to be realized, the Ego must learn Daimonese because, at first glance, the image may appear to be proverbial Greek, hopelessly undecipherable and, therefore, to be ignored. If not ignored, there is the impetus to give it a verbal rendition as quickly as possible with little or no processing. Our culture and lifestyle encourages this because words are efficient. We can transmit them quickly and they can be quickly recorded and understood by others.

The first step in learning Daimonese is to become not so quick to translate our images into words. We decipher their message by spending time with them and interacting with them, as illustrated in the following example.

The Truth About King Kong

The spiritual search begins in the confines of our own psyche. When we allow unstructured imagery to show up on our inner movie screen, we inevitably begin running into parts of ourselves that we ordinarily avoid, deny, or hide from the world and ourselves. Spirit recognizes the importance of seeking the divine with psychic wholeness, that is with inclusion of the parts of psyche that we would rather not acknowledge. An encounter with an inner entity at this level can be extremely moving and enlightening.

Jim was a young man whose poorly controlled temper was creating problems on the job and in his relationship with his girl friend. Throughout his life, friends and family had confronted him from time to time with his irritability and explosive reactions to minor stress.

When Jim sat across from me in the therapy hour he described himself as having been quick to anger as far back as he could remember. He expressed interest in change but said he did not know where to begin. He claimed to have no awareness of why he was so prone to overreact to people and situations.

We decided to use imagery as a means of helping him to get in touch with and hopefully better integrate the angry component of his personality. He knew it was there inside of him and that everyone around him had encountered it at some time or another. Now it was time for him to come face to face with it.

Relaxation did not come easy to Jim but with some work he was able to open himself up to imagery. It is then that I instructed him to invite his Unconscious to send him an image of the angry part of himself.

Instantly, a visualization of himself dressed in a gorilla suit came into his consciousness. Included in the image were other people in his life. They perceived him to be a genuine gorilla and were fleeing from him in terror.

Left alone, Jim attempted to get into dialogue with the gorilla suit but it was mute. It seemed to have no life of its own. It was animated only by the person inside.

Directly upon his return to ordinary consciousness, Jim reported a memory that he had not reviewed in many years. He recalled actually having been given a gorilla costume at Halloween when he was about six years old.

He went from door to door with other children in the neighborhood for Trick or Treat. His friends told him he looked scary and none of the neighbors recognized him when he appeared at their door. The occasion was great fun and he said the costume was the best he ever had.

That Halloween was the last special occasion on which Jim and his family were together. Before the following Thanksgiving his parents had separated and they were divorced a few months later.

At our next imagery session, Jim returned to the visualization of himself in the gorilla suit. I requested that he watch himself take it off and he complied. To his surprise, he did not find himself inside, at least not himself in his present state. Instead it was the little six year old Jim of the past. The child was shaking with fright.

Jim asked the child what was scaring him so and the child replied it was because he could hear his parents fighting almost every night. It was not unusual for his father to leave, slamming the door behind him, when the conflict reached its peak. The child said he knew the time would come when his father would not return.

As the dialogue continued it was apparent that little Jim's fear extended beyond the departure of his father. He dreaded being left alone with his loved but sickly and seemingly helpless mother. He knew he was going to have to take care of her and didn't feel big and strong enough to do the job.

This imagery quite accurately presented Jim's Angry Self and Inner Child as being one and the same and this brought new insight to him. Jim conversed with the Child who told him he had never recovered from his sadness over the family's dissolution and acknowledged he was still frightened by all kinds of responsibility.

The Halloween costume Jim wore had been discarded after October 31st but, following the divorce, he had put on a metaphorical King Kong suit that he had worn continuously. By adopting the countenance and manner of an untamed, angry beast, he had sought to protect himself and to let the world know that no one better bother him or his mother. This offense was his defense against his feelings of fear and inadequacy.

The imagery taught him that his aggressive attitude and behaviors were equivalent to a gorilla suit. More importantly, it showed that he was concealing from himself and the world the frightened little boy at the core of his being.

Later, when Jim began psychospiritual work his Daimon took the form of a gorilla named Pansy, a sweet natured but powerful creature. The imagery she generated taught more eloquently than any sermon the positive base of power.

Pansy transported Jim to her home, the African jungle. She took him to a shady, secluded spot near a plain on which a herd of gazelles was feeding. There in the shadows he saw a young gazelle that was lame and alone. She looked up at him through frightened eyes and he was filled with compassion.

Jim placed his arms around the frantic animal and could feel her heart pounding. With gentle strokes and soothing words, he calmed her. After a few moments, he was surprised to notice that her leg had become sound. Joyfully, he let her go and watched her run back to the herd.

Pansy instructed Jim that most of the people in the world were just like the little gazelle - frightened and wounded and in need of love to be healed. She told him he wasn't the only one with a scared little child within and that, if he would let it show more, others could feel compassion for that part of him just as he had felt it for the gazelle.

Within a couple of months, Jim's angry attitude was barely observable to himself or others.

A frequently observed phenomenon is demonstrated here.

Once we have begun working with our imaged Daimon, he or she is very apt to generate for us further imagery that teaches a needed lesson, confronts us with some important aspect of ourselves, promotes healing, demonstrates solutions to problems, or enables us to transcend space, time, energy, and matter. This makes learning to understand the language of imagery a worthwhile task indeed.

The Daimon On Pig Island

We might look upon inner imagery as something analogous to the private, thought form of Daimonese. A more public, outspoken form can be noted when the Daimon manifests himself through the agency of something in the external environment. My earlier account of my encounter with a hawk is an example of this.

A more unusual example appears in the story of Michael Rockert, inasmuch as the messenger was an inanimate object. This was a client who remembered clearly when and why he dissociated from his Daimon. He was a tall, dark man of thirty-three when he consulted me about his depressed state.

The most unusual feature of his condition was that he could find absolutely nothing in his life that was seriously unsatisfactory. He was secure in his job, headed for a top executive position in the next few years, and happily married with a four-year-old child. He was an avid golfer with a decent handicap and enjoyed satisfactory social relationships.

Michael thought it ironic that he was not finding enough meaning in these various aspects of his existence to make life vital and interesting. On the contrary, the rewards of his life were not compensating for its mundane stresses. At times he found himself wishing he could uproot and start over somewhere.

I asked this young man if there had ever been a time when life seemed like a great adventure to him. I wanted to know if being alive had on any occasion made him feel he was part of some important, unfolding drama.

Mike immediately recalled having had such feelings in his youth. He revealed a single incident in which that sense of participating in something grand and mystical came into full focus. He had never before spoken of the event to anyone.

It occurred when he was twelve years old and an acolyte at his parish church. At that time, along with his parents, he was an active participant in the life of the church though not intensely religious by nature. On the day in question he had an extraordinary experience.

It was Easter Sunday and he was the cross bearer, leading the choir and priests in procession to the high altar. The glorious music, the incense, the bright dancing flames atop the candles, and the presence of his parents and neighbors in the congregation converged to generate an exultant feeling in his breast as he led the celebrants into the church.

Arriving at the altar, he placed the staff topped with the golden cross on its stand and took his seat beside the other acolytes as the service began. Looking up at the cross he had carried, he saw that it was reflecting the light from the candles in an unusual way.

The reflection was as bright as sunlight - blinding. He wanted to look away but found he could not. The white light became iridescent and seemed to penetrate his body and mind, dazzling him. He felt dizzy, giddy, infused with some supernatural energy. When the spell was broken, he discovered to his surprise that a good ten minutes had passed.

At the end of the service, when the boy carried the cross once again during the recessional, he had a feeling of having been touched by the Divine. He had a sense of peace, of having received confirmation that his life was on the right track. It lasted for several months.

Just before his thirteenth birthday, Mike's mother was killed in a car crash while she was out shopping for his presents. His world was shattered. Deep, angry grief overtook him. The peace and joy that the Resurrection had left in his heart gave way to the pain and abandonment of his personal crucifixion.

Instead of trying to recapture the light, the youngster renounced it. He no longer trusted life or whatever force was in charge of it. He did not become rebellious - just indifferent. A condition of chronic, low-grade depression was established which followed him into adulthood.

It was the faint urging of his abandoned Daimon that brought him in to see me. "If this is all there is to life," the Daimon was saying, "it's hardly worth the effort."

Mike and I discussed what had happened to him in terms of his having developed a defensive denial of everything hopeful, wonderful, and magical about life. On his second visit, after reviewing his current state in the framework of denial, he made the following statement:

"When my mom died I was completely flooded with rage and fear. I felt physically sick all the time and just talking with people or doing ordinary things seemed like impossible demands. I distanced myself from the Church and all other institutions except school, which provided me with an excuse for staying withdrawn. I constantly fell back on the need to study. Who could fault that?

"I was in agony and, although it wasn't a conscious thing, I'm sure I decided to protect myself from ever having to face that kind of suffering and disappointment again. All of that elation I had felt during the year before mom's death intensified the pain so much that I vowed never to go back to the mountain top.

"So I sentenced the part of me you were talking about to the deepest, darkest dungeon of my mind. I was never ever going to let him color my perception of reality again. Life in the world for me was going to be somber, joyless, and monotonous no matter what happened. I guess where I'm at today is the consequence of that resolution."

With further discussion, Mike became interested in calling forth his Daimon but was adamant in his belief that he could not do so through imagining. He perceived himself to be totally lacking in imagery skills.

Seeking an alternative, we reflected together on the strong emergence of his sense of wonder at that Easter service years ago and concluded that some kind of ritual might help him make contact. Mike agreed but stated that, having withdrawn from the Church, he now found religious ritual to be too esoteric. He decided he could better connect with the metaphysical world through some more personal, visceral channel.

I suggested that he create a ritual of his own design and Mike became enthusiastic about it. After considering several possibilities, he decided he would take his boat out by himself for a day and cruise around some of the depopulated offshore islands. It would be for him a quest - he would invite his Daimon to direct the journey and would simply go wherever his intuition sent him.

Journeys of all kinds are excellent rituals for eliciting wonders, so I endorsed his plan. Neither of us had any idea of what, if anything, he might experience that would bring enchantment back into his life but we both felt it would be worthwhile.

For those who do not speak Daemonese the outcome of Mike's excursion will seem vapid and pointless. It will surely disappoint those who require mighty signs and heavy drama. Yet, it is quite exemplary of the simple ways by which the Daimon brings forth the metaphysical world in the natural world when allowed to lead.

When I saw my client the following week he looked more relaxed. His monotone had given way to more lilting speech.

Eager to give an accounting of his stress at the outset of his voyage, he spoke of nearly turning back right after leaving the dock. His left brain was telling him he was acting like an idiot. He was feeling angry with me for sanctioning such an inane activity.

Then, about twenty minutes into the cruise, a change came over him. He had a sense of being guided. He tried to slough it off as autosuggestion but could not. He was confident that, somehow, the trip was going to serve a purpose.

Mike spent the morning cruising around several of the numerous tiny islands that lie along the Gulf Coast of Florida. At noon, he ate a sandwich and drank a beer. By one o'clock, clouds were building and he knew he would have to head for port within an hour or so.

At this point, he felt strongly drawn to an island dead ahead. He recognized it as a strip of land the locals call Pig Island because boaters often stop there and leave their litter behind. It seemed an unlikely place to make a spiritual connection but he had contracted with himself to follow his intuition.

Cutting the motor and drifting toward the island, he could see it had heavy, bird-occupied vegetation framed by stretches of white sand beach. The scene might have been picturesque had it not been marred by a scattering of bottles, cans, and paper goods.

Of one thing he was certain. There was nothing remarkable about this place. He could discern no rationale for his desire to investigate it.

Tossing the anchor over the side, he jumped into the warm, shallow water and waded to the shore. There were no other boats in sight so he knew he had the place to himself. Except for occasional birdcalls and waves lapping at the shoreline, it was strangely quiet.

Mike felt he was looking for something but had no idea what. So, he decided to walk the length of the beach that was perhaps 150 yards. He had traveled about half way when he stopped in his tracks. For a moment he thought his mind might be playing tricks on him. But no, the faint sound of music was coming from somewhere nearby.

He quickly determined the sound was coming from a radio but thought it rather eerie since he was sure there was no one else on the island. Following his ears, he walked a short distance into the foliage where he discovered a small portable radio hanging on a mangrove branch, suspended by its carrying strap.

Obviously, the radio had been lost or left behind by a prior visitor though it was difficult to envision how this could have happened, especially with the instrument turned on. What struck him as extraordinary, however, was that when he reached it the song coming across the airways was "When You Wish Upon a Star."

The song brought him instantly to tears. It had been one of his mother's favorites. She had sung it to him many times when he was a child.

Mike took the radio and returned to his boat, feeling exhilarated. The environment had spoken to him in Daimonese. For him, the radio was a clear and sufficient sign. Its message, the song, was a call from his beloved, deceased mother telling him to believe. He was convinced he had been shown that the material universe can and will reveal its magical underpinning to those who are willing to see it.

Interestingly, an imaginary version of the radio became for Mike, who really did not visualize well, his guide when he did psychospiritual therapeutic work. He called the radio Jiminy (another of the Daimon's many faces) and carried on dialogues with it that helped him grow.

Rituals are an effective channel through which we can call forth the Daimon. They do not necessarily require incantations or special paraphernalia. They can be archaic, well-choreographed procedures or our own inventions. The only requirement is that we appoint the Daimon to be the master of ceremonies and interpret the experience in his language. This is what makes the difference between an odd occurrence of finding an abandoned radio on a deserted island and the magical event of receiving a message from an unseen source.

Is the latter interpretation sheer delusion? Is it nothing but the psychological fulfillment of an infantile wish?

There are those who would tell us Michael's visit to Pig Island was completely without meaning but Michael himself disagrees. His Daimon has remained free and active since that first journey and he has subsequently fulfilled his desire to have others join him in the performance of this spiritual rite.

He now repeats the boating ritual three or four times a year. His wife has joined him as a fellow seeker, as well as some close friends. They all claim to discover new wonders on every quest and Mike has suffered no recurrence of his depression.

In Daimonic language both Jim and Mike received instruction regarding what they needed to do in order to become whole and move closer to the Divine.

Jim needed to let go of his angry, aggressive defense and start loving the wounded child dwelling within him and others. Mike needed to restore his belief that there is "something more" to life than birth, suffering, and death. A source of wisdom not entirely of themselves knew just what they needed and presented the lesson through dramatic, deeply personal imagery. When the student is ready to learn, the teacher appears.

Doctor Daimon, I Presume

Sometimes individuals are awakened to their Daimon through its function as healer. Those who do not speak Daimonese may not recognize messages that could alleviate symptoms, cure disease, or even deliver them from the clutches of death.

Matthew Jessup was a dyed in the wool non-believer when I first met him. He was a man who had survived to middle age (quite nicely in his opinion) with no need to acknowledge, much less call upon, any of his sub-selves, especially one with metaphysical leanings. He had been programmed from childhood to believe that success in life is achieved by taking charge of everyone and everything in one's environment, working hard, and not getting bogged down by emotions. This formula served him very well until he was involved in an industrial accident that left him with a chronic pain problem and limited mobility.

Feelings, which in the past he had always been able to put out of awareness, began to torment him. He found himself depressed and, worse than that, unable to send his depression away.

The physician supervising his rehabilitation recognized Matt's emotional state and began treating him with anti-depressant medication. To the patient, taking the medicine was tantamount to publicly advertising his inadequacy. A real man, he thought, should be able to grit his teeth and carry on without any mind-altering drugs.

It should come as no surprise when I tell you that the first medication prescribed was not effective. Perceiving this as an unfavorable sign, his doctor referred him to me for psychotherapy.

Matt arrived at my office full of anger. Having to see a therapist was yet another blow to his already battered self-esteem. He had agreed to come in only because refusal to do so would affect his disability benefits.

He looked deflated when I strategically said at the end of our initial interview that I thought psychotherapy would be a long and difficult process because of his negative feelings about it. He looked instantly crestfallen, the response I fully anticipated. As I had hoped, my next statement perked him up considerably.

I expressed belief that he really was wanting to feel better and suggested there was something he could do which might eliminate the need for extensive therapy. His look of dismay relaxed a bit and I knew I had captured his interest.

I went on to propose that he allow me to contact his M.D. and request that he prescribe another anti-depressant to replace the currently ineffective one. In return, I asked that Matt do everything in his power to consciously control his negative attitude about the medicine during the first four weeks of taking it.

I also stipulated that he should see me weekly during those four weeks to do some related imagery work. I agreed that, if the medicine proved effective, I would inform his physician that he could just see me on an "as needed" basis. Of course, it was an offer this man could not refuse.

When I next saw him he had just started his new prescription without enthusiasm. He also began imagery work without enthusiasm.

His attitude was more positive after I suggested to him that within his body there was an incredible pharmacopoeia governed by an inner wisdom that knew just what he needed in order to reduce his symptoms. I guided him into a more relaxed state and encouraged him to invite an image representing this inner pharmacist to enter his consciousness.

Nothing happened for a while and Matt was beginning to show signs of restlessness when he said with genuine surprise, "Oh, here he comes now." Saying "This is wild", he went on to report that he was visualizing a small man with gray hair, a professorial type, seated on a stool in what was obviously a chemistry lab.

The lab was small but jammed with equipment. There were test tubes, flasks, and Bunsen burners. and other tools of the trade all about. The chemist was busy writing out some elaborate formula.

Matt had to be encouraged every step of the way but was too dumbfounded by his imagery to resist. Through dialogue Matt discovered his name was Dr. Hughes. Dr. Hughes identified himself as Matt's "Inner Healer".

I urged my client to question Dr. Hughes regarding the appropriateness of his new medication. Hughes replied that it was not exactly the formula that would work best for him.

I then suggested Matt ask the image if he could make the formula more effective by activating some natural body chemicals to make up for its deficiency. Hughes said that would be quite possible as long as Matt stayed on the basic drug as prescribed.

Upon return to ordinary consciousness, Matt was incredulous. He had started with no expectation of encountering any image of anything, much less that it would address the issue of his medication from a position in opposition to his conscious thinking.

By the following week, Matt was already displaying a slight alteration of his depressed mood. Moreover, he was quite taken by the imagery experience and really liked the idea that his mind/body system was playing an active part in his treatment rather than his being a passive recipient of some young doctor's cleverness. He confided that during his childhood Dr. Hughes had been a much-respected family physician.

There is no hard evidence to support that the imagery had anything to do with Matt's progress. As a matter of fact, his doctor attributed the abatement of Matt's depression to his having "hit upon" the right medication for his patient.

In the end, the greatest surprise was Matt's insistence that his awakening to his Inner Healer made all the difference. He requested extended therapy so that we could put Dr. Hughes to work on his pain. His request was granted and he succeeded in reducing his level of pain.

At our final therapy session Matt came in carrying a book and asked me if I thought it would help him to further develop his relationship with his Inner Healer. It was Jeanne Achterberg's (1985), Imagery in Healing. Being quite familiar with the book I unhesitatingly endorsed it. I had a sense that Matt had begun to speak Daimonese and was on a path that he would travel far.

CHAPTER EIGHT

Side Effects

We have some very superior blessings, too, but they're very little asked for.

- Gilbert and Sullivan
The Sorcerer

In the operetta called <u>The Sorcerer</u>, Gilbert and Sullivan (1968) comically examine the unexpected results that can occur when people turn to magic in order to adjust their lives. In the play, the townspeople secure the services of Mister John Wellington Wells, "a dealer in magic and spells," who addresses their need with a potion that produces consequences that are far different from what was expected.

Here in the Twenty-first Century, our magicians are frequently called "doctor" and their potions are called pharmaceuticals but we have not been completely delivered from unexpected consequences. Most of us are well aware that the magic pills may do the exact opposite of what they are intended to do and or produce their own array of new physiological sensations. The same is true for allhealing devices and techniques. They all have side effects - some benign, even enjoyable, and some not.

Connecting with the Daimon brings side effects which, while not in any way injurious, may be surprising and require some psychological adjustment even if welcomed.

In seeking the Divine, we subject ourselves to greater influence from the Divine. Our conscious will is weakened, sometimes broken. We, who began our quest as the pursuer, find ourselves pursued. Poet Francis Thompson (1941) recognized this phenomenon when he described God as "The Hound of Heaven," relentlessly tracking his quarry. Subtly, without our conscious consent, the side effects take hold.

One of the first noted is a modification in the way one views and interacts with the environment and its inhabitants. The physical world increasingly feels like a sacred place and all who journey spiritually in it seem to be, in the words of King David's well known psalm, "being followed by goodness and mercy." It is a bonus which may sometimes feel like an onus.

In this chapter we shall explore the ways in which those engaged in Daimonic work are pursued by goodness and mercy. We shall talk especially of the assaults of miracles, love, and forgiveness on spiritual seekers.

What The Fortune Cookies Teach

I am inordinately fond of Chinese food. I frequently wok cook at home and go to Chinese restaurants. On such occasions, the traditional fortune cookie at the end of the meal is a relished part of the fun.

The tiny strips of paper inside of the cookie usually contain forecasts of good luck but also, at times, bear statements of wisdom. I have collected some favorites through the years. Among them are the following:

1. To try is to do nothing.
2. The best way to study oneself is to forget oneself.
3. It does not matter how slowly you proceed so long as you do not stop.
4. In the silence you hear the most important things.
5. A hundred million miracles are happening every day.

This last one is my favorite. It is a Daimonic observation. Connecting with the Daimon is like being given a telescope which enables you to see that you are standing in the middle of a dazzling shower of meteors which has been raining without your awareness since the beginning of time. You are awed by the recognition that so much wonder has been escaping your attention.

Those who allow their Daimon to lead them toward the Gleam are pursued by miracles. They see the wonder and mystery in everyday events which others take for granted.

The dictionary tells us that a miracle is a marvelous event occurring through the intervention of some supernatural agency. The Daimon reminds us that this definition is made manifest in such happenings as birth, death, the sunrise, storms, spontaneous cures, the fertilization of an egg, the migration of birds, the change of seasons and many other familiar phenomena.

The Daimon maintains what the left brain would call a stupid belief. She believes that miracles happen spontaneously and frequently. No matter where she is, no matter where she goes, she expects to encounter miracles. Any plot of ground on which she stands is fertile ground for a wondrous event. This does not stem from an irrational belief that something extraordinary is guaranteed to take place everywhere she goes or on every occasion. It means that the potential for such an event is present at all times.

Lefty says this is stupid. It's all explainable. If not now, in due time. Eventually there will be no mysteries.

An interesting footnote is that the word "stupid" has its root in the Latin verb "stupere" meaning to strike senseless. When something "stupendous" takes place, a person is struck dumb, made inarticulate (stupid).

The Daimon is stupid, literally struck dumb by the miracles surrounding her. Unlike Lefty, she is not compelled to try to explain them. She subscribes to what is stated in A Course in Miracles (Foundation for Inner Peace, 1985): "Miracles are natural. When they do not occur something has gone wrong." (Text, page 1).

Those who are in dialogue with the Daimon are assured that life is going to afford them their share of extraordinary experiences. They are not likely to feel the urge to go running off to the site of someone else's miracle as soon as it is reported in the media.

In today's world we see many examples of people attempting to duplicate the personal experience of another because it has been labeled "miraculous." A small town widow has a vision of the Virgin Mary and the sleepy thoroughfares of that place are soon jammed with people hoping to get a peek at the widow or her apparition before they know anything of the woman or the circumstances. There is no Daimonic guidance here, just thrill seeking or an attempt to claim an easy mystical experience.

The Daimon can and will direct us to sacred places to feed the soul and bring us closer to the Gleam. Perhaps for some individuals a journey to India is essential but for most of us a special spot in our own backyard can do as much.

Many Westerners find themselves attracted to the religions and philosophies of the East and some engage in serious study of them. While this is a legitimate calling, there is the added difficulty of surmounting the cultural and linguistic foundation on which they rest. Some of their attraction is based on the erroneous belief that the two great Western religions, Judaism and Christianity, do not have a strong mystical tradition. In fact, both have bodies of literature and time honored rituals that support mystical experience but these are not widely promoted by the modern Institutional Church.

In or out of the Church, those on the path to the Gleam recognize that they are engulfed by miracles. Prominent among everyday miracles is the occurrence of love.

Love Vigilance

Love vigilance is similar to the Daimon's expectation of miracles. She is ever mindful of the potential for love, a miraculous happening in itself, to develop any time, anywhere, with anyone.

Science has advanced us to the point of being able to identify and name most of the great forces at work in the universe but has not gotten around to explaining some of them very clearly. Electricity is one example; love is another.

Volumes have been written and spoken about love but no consensus definition has been derived from that abundant verbiage. Love seems to defy rational explication.

We "know" love through the workings of our entire body/mind system. We symbolize it with an image of the heart as if to concede that our brains are incapable of fathoming it. We create stories, poems, songs, and works of art extolling the pleasure and pain associated with it but the actual experience of it remains ineffable.

We are free to choose from a variety of models that have been set forth regarding the origin of love. My bias is that love is something innate in the human organism. It is an archetypal presence when we emerge from the birth canal, waiting to be actualized as soon as we can distinguish self from other. Once awakened, it will recur again and again in our lifetime. We cannot prevent its beginning and we cannot make it stay once begun. Love happens to us.

Tragically, many of us have experiences (often our earliest ones) which interfere with the happening of love. Through such experiences we come to associate love with unbearable pain or deep sadness. We develop psychological and social defenses designed to protect us from ever reliving the suffering which our attempt to love or be loved inflicted on us.

We pay a heavy price for this protection in the form of emotional insulation. We sacrifice spontaneity of feeling and the Daimon becomes an immediate casualty. Once the practice of love vigilance is deemed to be not safe, the Daimon must be cloistered on the Shadow side.

When free, the Daimon frequently reminds us that love happens. He does not expect it to occur on a personal level with everyone he meets but he does not exclude the possibility of it happening with anyone including those who at first are disliked. He is attuned to its emergence and responds to it appreciatively, even reverently, whether it takes the form of sexual love, spiritual, parental, fraternal, or friendship.

Love fertilizes the soil in which miracles grow. If everyone we encounter on our daily journey, including those with whom we are in conflict, is met with openness and acceptance because they are potential objects of our love, surprising consequences can ensue as exemplified in the following clinical episode.

The Bitchy Old Woman: A Love Story

Several years ago, I was supervising a talented young clinical social worker whom we shall call Rhoda. For the first time in her career she was working with a geriatric patient with no family. The woman had been admitted to a nursing care facility following hip surgery and was facing the prospect of having to give up her modest little house in favor of continuing custodial care.

Upon admission to the care unit this eighty-two year old woman with a history of never having been a shrinking violet became wild as a coot, displaying opposition and hostility to everyone who crossed her path. In her worst moments she would throw things from her bedside table about the room and unleash torrents of four letter words on her caretakers. She refused to discuss business affairs or a life plan with anyone.

Poor Rhoda was called in by Billie's physician to get her to settle down and accept her fate. At their first meeting, the fiercely independent counselee declared she wasn't going to let some "fat, pimply faced, teen aged social worker" tell her what to do. (Rhoda was slightly overweight and didn't have the clearest complexion but she was in her mid twenties.)

Hurt and angered by Billie's caustic comments, Rhoda consulted with members of the staff, all of whom confirmed that the client treated them similarly. They were uniformly hostile toward her and one person said she wished the old bitch were on life support so she could unplug her.

Rhoda brought the situation to her supervisory hour, requesting my input. After listening, I asked if she believed it could ever be possible for love to happen between her and Billie.

"Are you kidding?" she asked loudly.

"No," I said seriously. "It isn't that I think you have to love her in order to connect with her but I think you have to believe that's a possibility in order to connect with her. It looks to me like she's thrown down the gauntlet to everyone, daring them to find her soft spot. I think you might start by addressing the issue of her loveableness or lack thereof so she can see that you at least are seeking a way."

Rhoda, newly acquainted with her Daimon, perceived an inner voice encouraging her to do something creative with Billie. At their next meeting she walked in and told Billie she had been hurt by her remarks during their first encounter and had walked away "mad as hell." She divulged that she had thought about getting off the case but had come back because she was not content to let her first impression be her only one. Looking Billie in the eye she stated forcefully that she intended to find something about her which she could love.

The octogenarian's eyes twinkled with amusement. She said simply, "Well, girlie, let me know when you do."

Rhoda said, "I promise," and went on to ask Billie how in the hell she thought she was going to take care of herself at home. She said she had been thinking she could admire Billie's spunk but it was hard to tell where that ended and obstinacy began.

Rhoda was amazed by the response. The old one announced that she knew quite well she could no longer live independently. She didn't think she was going to live much longer anyway and was reconciled to dying in custodial care. She said all of the fuss about getting out was so she could take care of Felicity.

"And who is Felicity?" asked Rhoda.

"My cat. My best friend," came the reply.

It was revealed that Felicity had been Billie's closest companion for twelve years. After her fall, the next door neighbors had agreed to take care of the cat until her owner returned. They were nice people but not especially fond of animals and Billie surmised they were getting tired of being foster parents. She wanted to go home, claim her pet who was old and not in good health and take her to the veterinarian to be put to sleep. Until this was accomplished, she had no intention of either dying or settling down.

Rhoda, herself the owner of an adored feline, was suddenly filled with compassion. "Why didn't you explain this instead of carrying on so?" she asked.

"I did, sister," Billie crackled, "and everybody including my doctor said I shouldn't be worrying about a silly cat. That's when I decided they were all ass holes and I told them they were. I knew there was no reasoning with people like that so I started kicking butt."

Rhoda had to suck in her lip to cover up a smile of approval. Love happens.

At that moment, the two women bonded. Rhoda promised Billie that to the best of her ability she would see to it that her wishes regarding Felicity were carried out. She made contact with the neighbors who, in fact, were anxious to get rid of their four legged border. Then, she scheduled an appointment with a veterinarian of Billie's choice.

Knowing how much it would mean to her client, Rhoda took responsibility for personally picking up the animal, which proved to be thin and frail. Having made special arrangements, enroute to the vet's office she stopped at the care facility where the long time companions had an opportunity to spend half an hour in close embrace and to say good-bye. Rhoda wept unabashedly as she gently removed Felicity from her tearful owner's arms.

At their next meeting, Rhoda reported that Felicity had received her injection serenely and had peacefully departed from life before the needle was withdrawn. Billie smiled, expressed heartfelt appreciation, and said they could get on with the business of settling her affairs.

"Before we do," said Rhoda, "I want you to know I love you for the way you love Felicity and the way you stood up for her. I told you I was going to find something to love about you and I have."

The client's expression was serene, her manner soft. "You're a kind person, girlie. If I was going to be around for very long I'd want you for my friend. As it is, we'll just finish our business together."

After that, Billie was no more trouble to her caretakers, most of whom started to find a little enjoyment in her hard edged humor.

Shortly after her affairs were in order, Billie developed a respiratory ailment. A series of complications followed and eight weeks later she died.

Rhoda had remained in periodic contact with Billie and saw her briefly just two days before her demise. All of her ferociousness was gone. She was uncomfortable and didn't want to talk much but before her visitor left she made a point of saying she was "just about ready to get out of this miserable nursing home and get my cat back."

Rhoda knew Billie was completely lucid and understood exactly what she meant. She smiled at her and said, "Go for it."

Billie holds a special place in Rhoda's heart to this day. As long as love is possible, anything is possible.

The God-Like Power

Another goodness that pursues those connected with the Daimon is the call to forgive. It is the Daimon's way of keeping the baggage light for the journey.

In most institutional religions members are called upon to believe certain doctrines concerning the nature of god and to worship him/her in prescribed ways. The God of Judaism and Christianity is no exception. The individual's duty to God and to fellow humans is defined. Some sects, such as Christianity, cite a duty to forgive, among others.

Duty or not, institutions that preach forgiveness are reminding us that human beings are empowered to do something that elevates them to the stature of a god. Man, as well as god, has the power to forgive.

We are not talking here about offering or accepting apologies. We are not talking about uttering the words, "I forgive you." We are talking about a profound, internal letting go.

There is no miracle when forgiveness is declared by someone who believes he is performing a magnanimous act of spiritual generosity that will allow another to feel excused or dissipate guilt. This is a pompous burlesque of true forgiveness.

Forgiveness is not doing someone else a favor. It is not enacted toward the end of assuaging someone's guilt although coincidentally it may have this effect.

Forgiveness is a gift to one's self. It frees us from the burden of judgment and internalized hurt and anger.

It does not carry the stipulation that we must like or approve of another's wrong actions. It does not demand that we passively "put up with" future actions of the same nature. It does not entail stuffing hurt and bitterness down into one's gut while pretending to be not offended.

In basic terms, forgiveness says, "What is done cannot be undone. Therefore, I am choosing to let it go." If we are serious about forgiving, it is an act that we shall perform over and over in our lifetime.

We have noted that the loving person is not one who loves everyone but rather one who is open to the possibility of love with everyone. Similarly, the forgiving person is not necessarily one who has forgiven everyone for everything but rather one who is willing to forgive. There are forgiving people who have not yet gotten around to forgiving all.

The fact remains that we can forgive anyone or anything we choose to forgive. The act of forgiving is distinguishable from acts of masochism, which is a pathological desire to suffer physical or emotional pain.

Even as we forgive others, we can assert our right to distance ourselves from them for the pain they have caused or might cause in the future. Forgiveness does not prohibit us from protecting ourselves from those who would do us harm.

As noted above, Christians proclaim that we have a bounden duty to forgive. For me, this sets up an obstacle to true forgiveness and increases the likelihood of it coming from the lips rather than the heart. In truth, we don't have to forgive anything. It is a matter of choice and therein lies its wonder.

This makes forgiveness a gift freely given. There are no strings attached.

Our capacity for forgiving may be the most convincing evidence of the Divine dwelling within us. Remember that it was Jesus' talk of forgiving which sent his Jewish contemporaries into orbit. He said and did lots of things they regarded as shocking and/or blasphemous but this is what took the cake.

The Judaic teaching at that time was that only God could forgive sins. The message of the God/Man was that we are all God/people. He was sent from God to tell us we are all sent from God. He declared that we can all forgive and be forgiven. The Kingdom is within us.

Forgiveness facilitates miracles. When we forgive we feel wonder-full. We are freed from festering emotional sores. We are cleansed and unburdened. Barriers between others and ourselves are removed.

The miracles begotten through forgiveness have never been stated more clearly and eloquently than in A Course in Miracles:

"What could you want forgiveness cannot give? Do you want peace? Forgiveness offers it. Do you want happiness, a quiet mind, a certainty of purpose, and a sense of worth and beauty that transcends the world? Do you want care and safety, and the warmth of sure protection always? Do you want a quietness that cannot be disturbed, a gentleness that never can be hurt, a deep, abiding comfort, and a rest so perfect it can never be upset?

"All this forgiveness offers you, and more. It sparkles on your eyes as you awake, and gives you joy with which to meet the day. It soothes your forehead while you sleep, and rests upon your eyelids so you see no dreams of fear and evil, malice and attack. And when you wake again, it offers you another day of happiness and peace. All this forgiveness offers you, and more." (Workbook for Students, page 213)

Out Of The Phantom's Clutches

There is an interesting sequel to a clinical story which I began in my earlier work, Imaginative Healing (Middleton, 1993). It illustrates how beneficial forgiveness can be to the forgiver.

The client in this story is thirty-one year old Jerry who consulted me because he was suffering from panic attacks. He was besieged by the occasional image of a pair of disembodied male hands that, in spite of his attempts to avoid it, always aroused acute anxiety.

In the course of our therapeutic work, Jerry decided to work with the troubling imagery but when he stood his ground and faced the hands they grabbed hold of him and began beating him viciously. This devastating visualization put him in touch with an incident that had occurred when he was about five years old. The memory had been stored for years in a dark corner of his mind.

He recalled being a little boy and wanting his father's attention. Father was seated in his favorite chair reading the newspaper and being non-responsive. So, Jerry flung himself into his father's lap.

To his shock and surprise, his dad became instantly enraged. He angrily hurled Jerry onto the sofa and began beating him with his fists.

It came to light that this was one of many similar reactions he had received at the hands of his alcoholic father who was killed while driving under the influence when Jerry was seven. He had successfully repressed all of those painful experiences with the help of his mother who, thinking it would do no harm to the child, told him repeatedly that his father had been a loving husband and kind, caring parent.

Jerry courageously allowed his repressed feelings into his consciousness with the intention of integrating them. At the first level of feeling, he was filled with abject despair over not being loved as he needed to be by this first, all-important man in his life.

As layers of emotion were peeled away, he got in touch with an aggressive urge to do violence back to his father. He entertained images of beating him bloody and throwing him out of the house.

Finally, he reached bedrock, recognizing that his father was a severely damaged human being who no longer had any power over him. At this point, he began to talk forgiveness.

The earlier account of Jerry's story concluded with the report that he was still in therapy and showing signs of improvement. I can now add to that a remarkable feature of his treatment.

You see, all the while Jerry was working through layers of feeling, the image of his father's hands continued to pop up unbidden. Each time, they would grab him once again and he would relive the old fear as strongly as ever.

When he began to consider the possibility of forgiving his father, he noticed a curious change in the hands. It was subtle at first and he could only say, "they look different," though they behaved the same. Then, came the a-ha.

"Those are no longer my father's hands!" he exclaimed during one of our imagery sessions. "Those are my hands! I've been saying he no longer has any power over me and this proves it's true. It's me that's doing the holding on. It's me! I'm continuing to beat up on myself and scare myself. It isn't him at all."

It was a breakthrough moment that spurred Jerry on to his act of forgiveness, which he now understood to be very literally a letting go. He did not need release from his father. He needed release from himself.

When the hands next appeared, they did not attack. Jerry stayed with the image and spoke to his father from his heart of hearts.

"I forgive you," he said tearfully. "I truly forgive you. From this moment on I am releasing you from responsibility for my pain and I am refusing to inflict further pain on myself."

The hands fluttered briefly before his eyes and faded out of sight. This was several years ago. They have not returned.

CHAPTER NINE

The Healing Gift

...the little girl did not know of the wonderful power the Silver Shoes gave her.

> - L. Frank Baum
> The Wizard of Oz

The Daimon comes to us bearing magical gifts. Chief among these are healing, creativity, soul nurturing, and mythologization. Each of these will be discussed in separate chapters.

Healing abilities are functions with which everyone is endowed and which are enhanced by the Daimonic connection. Whether we are healing or being healed, these abilities seem to be most powerfully present when we are in an altered state of consciousness.

Hildegard of Bingen who gained much notoriety as a healer in the Twelfth Century began in childhood to exhibit trance-like states in which she envisioned a dazzling white light that she called the "reflection of the living Light." This seems to have been the Gleam to which she was drawn throughout her long and holy life.

The once famous Andrew Jackson Davis, known as the Poughkeepsie Seer, who was credited with extraordinary healing power during the middle 1800's reported having interacted with Galen during a trance experience at age nineteen. His better known successor, Edgar Cayce, made his epiphany as a healer when he was sixteen and was struck by a baseball at the base of his spine. After the injury, he began behaving erratically at home and was sent to his room whereupon he fell into a deep sleep.

While his parents anxiously stood over him, a voice which seemed to emanate from the depths of his body ordered his mother to make a special poultice and place it on the back of his head. By morning he was back to normal but had no memory of what was apparently an appearance of his Inner Healer. This same Daimonic entity was destined to become a healing adviser to countless numbers of people during the remainder of Cayce's life.

When young Bernadette Soubirous dug into the earth she released a spring of magical waters which were to be instrumental in healing many of those who have sought them out at Lourdes. Bernadette's actions were directed by an image she called "The Lady" and which came to be identified as the Virgin Mary.

Sometimes the Daimon communicates more subtly as the small voice of intuition. This was what guided writer and editor Norman Cousins (1979) during his well known 1964 bout with ankylosing spondylitis, a form of arthritis that affects the body's connective tissue resulting in severe debilitation and usually death. Cousins believed that positive emotions like love, hope, laughter, and faith could heal his body and persuaded his doctor to let him leave the hospital and move into a hotel room where he assumed an active role in his own healing, devoting much time to humorous films and books. His rate of recovery was remarkable and eventually near total.

Healers (whether of self, others, or both) uniformly experience themselves as instruments. The common denominator is their sense of being directed or controlled by some force greater than themselves though the force is imaged in many different forms.

I call this the Daimonic force. The Daimon heals as he leads.

Healing and Treatment

I say with caution that the Daimon has a deep understanding of your mind/body system and has the power to promote healing. The caution is for those who may be inclined to expect him to raise fallen arches, straighten teeth, correct vision, or make hair grow on a bald spot.

When we talk of healing we must be clear about what we mean. Healing is not the same as treatment. If healing cures what ails your body (and that is not out of the question) that is incidental.

Healing refers to establishing wholeness. Wholeness, in turn, is related to holiness. To be healed is to be whole, to be connected in body, mind, and spirit. Healing is a psychospiritual endeavor.

Our cultural bias is to think of healing primarily in terms of correcting physical problems. This represents a confusion of the term with the notions of treatment and cure. Cure is a scientific/medical concept describing the eradication of disease and/or symptoms related to bodily impairment.

Treatment encompasses methods applied toward the goal of cure. It connotes the application of certain procedures such as surgery or the giving of medicine to someone who is sick or injured. Treatment is administered from the outside.

Healing is a process that takes place within an individual. Treatment usually promotes healing but healing is not solely dependent on treatment.

Historically, the scientific approach to treatment and cure has minimized or negated the value of healing. The clinical success of the scientific approach has been impressive and advancements have been made at an astonishing rate. Workers in the medical field are single mindedly devoted to the maintenance and restoration of bodily health. They look upon chronic suffering and death as failures of their cause.

Healers have a different perspective. Throughout their history they too have applied drugs and procedures to ailing parts of the body but their primary goal has been to ensure that the patient is in full possession and awareness of his spirit, thus making him whole. Continuing symptoms and even death do not constitute failure but continuing fragmentation of the individual does.

In most cases it is expected that the establishment of wholeness will diminish or eliminate symptoms and prolong life. However, the healer knows that death comes eventually, even to the most perfected human being. Therefore, to die is not the ultimate tragedy. To live or die in a state of disunity is a very great tragedy.

From the standpoint of the healer a person may be healed though continuously afflicted by a serious disease such as arthritis or diabetes. Carried to its logical conclusion, this definition allows us to be healed as we wait at death's door.

Healing favors use of the natural protective and corrective functions with which the mind/body system is endowed. This includes drawing upon our indwelling pharmacopoeia that is capable of rendering a biochemical response to almost any malfunction that arises. The Daimon is aware of, respects, and believes in this natural healing power but knows that complete healing goes far beyond the alleviation of symptoms or the cure of a single disease.

The EMT

I was privy to a remarkable example of healing a few years ago. The Inner Healer took the form of a Daimonic image and presented himself to the person involved who was an adolescent named Tom. He and his family had been in therapy with me about a year prior to the incident I'm about to recount.

Tom was not a bad kid but was definitely a free spirit.

A fire raged within him that could only be quenched by high excitement. He loved to take risks, to confront danger, and to be the first among his peers to do whatever. His father, an ex-marine, admired this quality and unconsciously encouraged Tom's wild side. His mother worried.

The family work we did strengthened their bonds and helped them to establish a workable set of rules and expectations with their teenager. Tom's rambunctious nature was not altered.

On the positive side, this youngster was bright and sensitive to the feelings of others. He was quick to become the champion of those whom he deemed to be oppressed.

Therapy with the family had been terminated for several months when I received a call from Tom's mother telling me that her son had been involved in an accident on his motorcycle and was seriously injured. His right leg had been broken in several places and he was scheduled for surgery the following day. She added that the doctors were not giving any guarantee that his leg could be saved.

I was a bit surprised when she indicated that Tom had requested a visit with me prior to going to the operating room but assured her I would arrange to do so. I ended up in his room just a short time before the scheduled procedure.

The young man, displaying cuts, bruises, and abrasions, was showing some effects from sedation but was quite lucid and smiled at me when I approached. He said he wished he had listened to me more carefully when I talked during therapy about his excessive need to take chances. He had been speeding on a curve when he flipped his bike.

I told Tom I was pleased that he had asked to see me but was curious as to why. He told me that right after he was brought to the Emergency Room and given pain medication he had seen a vision that was incredibly vivid. It was like a dream only he was sure he was awake. Recalling that we had done a little work with imagery last year, he thought I would be the best person to talk to about it. Almost apologetically, he said he thought it was very important to talk about it.

I stood close beside the bed and said I would be pleased to discuss the imagery with him. He then gave the following account:

"I was lying on the stretcher and, although nobody had said anything, I knew my leg was in really bad shape. I wanted to do something to help my leg but I figured it was out of my hands.

"All of a sudden, I got this picture of myself standing on a bridge. Something was coming at me out of the sky. I think it was an airplane. It crashed real close to me and knocked me over. Then, a big piece of metal came down on my leg.

"Well, I was soon aware of a lot of people standing around but none of them knew what to do. Somebody pulled the metal off of me and a guy who said he was a doctor walked over and looked at me. He just shook his head and said he couldn't do anything until he got me to a hospital.

"I was panicked because I knew that leg better start healing right away or it was just going to die. Then, I looked up and saw this young, strong guy standing over me.

"He was an EMT. He told me to not be afraid. He said the doctors would fix my leg at the hospital but, meanwhile, he was going to inject some very tiny EMT's into my leg. They would go inside and start doing all the preliminary work necessary to keep my leg alive. He produced a needle and, I guess, popped it into my leg. I don't know because I didn't feel anything.

"But right away I got a picture of these little guys picking up little bits of bone, vacuuming up blood spills, and keeping the area real clean. It was so reassuring. I dropped right off to sleep.

"Every time I've waked up I've looked in on these little EMT's and they're busy at work. They wave at me and tell me to relax. What do you think that is?"

Somewhat awed by the powerful symbolism, I said, "Well, Tom, I believe the EMT on the bridge was an image of a part of you I call the Inner Healer. We all have one. It's a part of us that knows how to activate all the powerful healing mechanisms that are built into our mind/body system. I think the little guys inside are images of those healing mechanisms in action. They are carrying out the directives of your Inner Healer. He wants you to know about this and take comfort in it."

"I sure do," he said, relaxing and beginning to drift into sleep.

I confirmed for Tom what he already believed was happening but also had doubts about. Perceiving me as a kind of imagery expert, he was able to accept my interpretation as a validation of his deep beliefs.

The surgery on his leg was extensive but quite successful. His post-operative rehabilitation proceeded much faster than normal according to his therapists. Most remarkable of all, however, was the change of attitude and behavior that followed.

Tom remained action oriented and assertive but lost his reckless abandon. Out of the blue he became interested in working with handicapped children, helping them to perform tasks which they found difficult and scary. He claimed that his reverence for his own body and for even more dysfunctional bodies had begun with the appearance of that lifesaving EMT on his imaginary bridge.

I would classify Tom's experience as a healing. His Daimon in the form of that EMT gained ascendancy at a time of crisis and put his healing skills to work. He also immediately began to lead Tom toward the Gleam.

Perhaps, as indicated by the bridge in the vision, Tom was already at a point of crossing over, making some significant changes in his way of being in the world. The plane or whatever it was falling out of the sky is reminiscent of the way an act of God is often depicted in stories and mythology. It brings to mind St. Paul being struck from his horse on the way to Damascus.

There is no hard evidence to support the idea that Tom's imagery had any effect on his healing. We can only say that it came at a time when many variables were converging to transform him. It also brings into focus for reflection the idea that illness, injury, and symptoms of every kind are harbingers of and catalysts for change.

A Message From The Neck

The notion of symptoms as messages deserves a little more development. Much of the Daimon's strength as healer lies in her gift for decoding symptom messages and addressing the issues that underlie them. Symptoms arise not just to announce that some particular organ or physiological function is out of whack, but that something in our bio-psycho-social-spiritual life needs attention as well. This orientation is the foundation of healing as opposed to treating.

To illustrate, I bring you Anita, a client who had suffered a mild neck injury prior to beginning therapy. She had backed her car into her curbside garbage container while pulling out of her driveway. On impact, she applied the brakes so forcefully that it caused her neck to snap. Her doctor prescribed temporary use of a collar and expected her to have a speedy recovery but her pain persisted in the absence of any identifiable medical condition.

When Anita came to see me, I was struck by her good looks and vivacious manner. In keeping with her status as a professional woman, she was stylishly dressed though her appearance was somewhat marred by the neck collar she claimed to still need for pain relief.

After a couple of exploratory sessions, I taught Anita a relaxation method and suggested that, while in a relaxed state, she ask her Unconscious to send her an image which would represent her neck pain. I warned her that the image might not seem immediately relevant but that she should accept without censorship whatever appeared.

The warning was well taken. She laughed to find herself visualizing a beat up old car that she guessed to be a vintage of the seventies.

Right away Anita said, "This is stupid."

Imagery work has taught me to have great faith that there is meaning in what appears on the client's inner movie screen no matter how unrelated the image seems to be. I asked her to put herself in the picture with the car and to focus on what she felt like doing. She immediately found a steel rod and began bashing the vehicle vigorously. This imagined activity became more and more intense. Before she was done, she had reduced it to a pile of rubbish.

Following this visualization, which surprised the client who perceived herself to be non-aggressive, we began to explore its meaning and possible connection to her neck pain. Her first line of defense was to call the episode "a meaningless example of overactive imagination," but I exhorted her not to settle for that.

Next, she came up with a superficial interpretation. Since she had been in a car when she hurt her neck, perhaps she was striking back at one in order to release all the pain and anger tied up in her injury.

With some more work it dawned on Anita that the car she had imaged was very similar to the car owned by Nick, her steady boyfriend in high school. Though her parents did not approve of him, he was her first love and her first sex partner.

She and Nick had spent many hours sitting in that car kissing and petting and, on Homecoming night, it was the place where they engaged in intercourse, the first time for her. She returned home past curfew on that occasion, feeling extremely guilty and found, to her horror, her parents waiting up in the living room. Noting his daughter's smeared make-up and disheveled appearance, the father launched an angry tirade, accusing Anita of no longer being a virgin. The girl denied the charge but had a prolonged battle with guilt thereafter. Eventually her guilt contributed to the break-up of her relationship with Nick.

In the light of this recall the client concluded that her imagined demolishing of the car was probably based on her desire to destroy the evidence of her sexual misbehavior. I supported this insight and asked her to look at how it might relate to her current pain problem. She spent a few moments in silent thought and burst into tears. She had arrived at the real source of her pain.

Anita acknowledged that a very attractive man with whom she worked had been coming on to her for the last couple of months. She was sexually excited by his interest but did not want to do anything to hurt her husband or jeopardize their marriage. Nevertheless, she agreed on one occasion to drive to a waterfront park after work and talk with her admirer. At that time they sat in his car and ended up doing some heavy petting. She found the experience intensely pleasurable but vowed to herself that it must not happen again.

It was on the day following this encounter that my client injured her neck. The injury made it easy for her to decline her co-worker's continuing bids for another meeting. The collar made it obvious that she was in no shape for trysting.

As long as the pain persisted, Anita felt justified in continuing to wear the collar. With it on, she felt reassured that it would be apparent to everyone that she literally could not be "necking." In addition, the pain served as fit punishment for her marital transgression.

Once the young woman got all of this in focus she became aware that the continuance of her pain carried a significant psychological payoff. For guidance regarding what to do, she consulted her Daimon, a Siamese cat named Tuptim. With Tuptim's help she finally reached a firm decision and emphatically informed her seducer that she wanted nothing more to do with him. Within a couple of weeks she felt confident about persevering and her "pain in the neck" subsided.

In this case, the individual's pain was transmitting an urgent message. It was saying, "You need to do more than just deal with me. You need to take yourself out of a situation that is causing you guilt and stress. You need not to destroy the evidence but rather to take charge of the problem."

Healing Relationships

My role with Anita and other clients written about in this book might be described as that of a facilitator of healing, someone who helps another to activate and make use of their own healing power.

I know from experience that I can benefit from medical treatment dispensed by someone who is relatively cold, impersonal, or even unpleasant. As long as I don't allow that person's way of being to contaminate for me the medicine or procedure they apply, I can integrate his or her contribution as something beneficial and augment it with my innate healing power.

Conversely, treatment administered in a caring, loving manner by someone I respect has much more potency. It not only has the potential to cure me but it confirms and strengthens the part of me that feels valuable and loveable. I am simultaneously cured and healed.

If I am to promote healing in others, I believe I must, first of all, be reasonably whole. I say reasonably whole because total, integrated wholeness is probably not a state achieved by ordinary human beings in a single lifetime.

Rarely does anyone rise above the afflictions of life to the extent of being unlimited by them. We are all covered with scars. Healers like everyone else are wounded but, ideally, they maintain the integrity of their basic sense of worth and are able to administer unto themselves.

If I bring this relative wholeness into a relationship with another for the purpose of facilitating healing, I must encounter this person as someone whom I am willing to love. Carl Rogers (1951) displayed his genius when he designated the cornerstone of therapy to be the therapist's "unconditional positive regard" of the client. The person to be healed must be perceived as someone worthy of love and attention.

With this attitudinal overlay in place, what I say and do within the framework of the particular school of therapy to which I ascribe is somewhat incidental as long as it is structured to empower and enable the Inner Healer of the other person to do her work. This is most likely to occur if, in a spirit of trust and caring, I bring to our encounter my authentic, involved presence.

Sometimes, this is absolutely all I have to offer a suffering client. There are times when I find myself totally at a loss in regard to what to do at the moment for someone awash in a sea of misery.

In this context, I recall a young woman named Tammy who came to her therapy session in a state of utter devastation, holding in her trembling hands a note from her lover. It tersely stated that, for a long while, he secretly had loved someone else and that he had left the area to be with that person.

Tammy had no prior awareness of his situation and was taken completely by surprise. Her agony was so overwhelming that she threw herself on the floor of my office and curled up in a fetal position.

"Help me!" she screamed. "You've got to do something! You're my therapist! What are you going to do to help me?"

I was stymied. I wanted desperately to alleviate her suffering but had no notion of how to do it.

Finally, I said to her, "I'm going to sit here beside you for the next hour while you feel your pain in whatever way you need to."

The statement sounded pretty feeble to me and I felt woefully inadequate. Nevertheless, I followed through, placing a hand on her hand and saying very little.

We sat this way the entire hour and Tammy wept buckets. When time was up, she allowed me to call her best friend and arrange for her to spend the night. We also made another appointment for the next day.

A couple of weeks later when some of her grief had subsided, Tammy and I were discussing her progress. In the midst of this, she referred back to that awful day and thanked me for that session. She said it was one of the most comforting experiences of her life.

"Nothing on earth could have helped me more," she declared, "than being able to cry my heart out in a safe place with someone who cared." What I had perceived as doing very little, she received as powerful healing.

I realized that, on my side, my Ego had felt unable to cope with the situation and I had shifted into an altered state of consciousness. My Daimon, with great understanding, had come up with just the right thing to do to facilitate Tammy's healing.

It is a lesson worth remembering. While treatment relentlessly involves doing this, that, or the other thing to or for the patient, the healing process involves journeying with the patient who may sometimes need to backtrack, stop, or regroup as she seeks to claim parts of herself which have been mangled, lost, or denied.

The Most Powerful Thing

In the motion picture, <u>Who Framed Roger Rabbit</u> (Disney, 1988), the title character proclaims, "A laugh can be a very powerful thing." Norman Cousins (1979) gave us empirical verification of that statement.

In mankind's never ending search for elixirs and potions with magical effect, there has been a tendency to overlook some of the most available yet most wonderful healers of all. Only recently has aspirin been accorded its rightful place as a miracle medicine, likewise for humor.

The Daimon is quite aware of the healing and rehabilitative power of humor and makes liberal use of it. This is not to say the Daimon is a stand-up comedian.

His special gift allows us to see and respond to the humor that is the understructure of the comedy called life. He helps us plug into the funny side of ourselves, others, and the various situations with which we are confronted, especially in our darkest moments. Sometimes he brings us laughter that is sprinkled with tears, sometimes it is pure slapstick, sometimes it is socially or politically incorrect, but at its core it is always compassionate.

As a traveler in the spirit realm, the Daimon more than any other part of us is aware of the contrast between the divinity and baseness woven into our human fiber. He can laugh at the great cosmic joke which places human beings somewhere on a continuum between the Godhead and dog do-do.

We are ridiculous beings in an improbable universe and awareness of this will keep our sense of humor alive.

Nothing is more healing than finding some gentle humor when we are overtaken by the fearful shadow of death. Death and loss are always tragic but the first ripples of laughter are as sure a sign of grief's impermanence and rebirth's imminence as the robin's song is a harbinger of spring.

Touching on this subject never fails to bring to my mind a marvelous episode of the <u>Mary Tyler Moor Show</u>, an outstanding television series of the 70's. This particular show entitled "Chuckles Bites the Dust" and written by David Lloyd (1975), is about an entertainer known as Chuckles the Clown who is killed when he goes to a parade dressed as a peanut and an elephant attempts to shell him.

Throughout the episode Mary is incensed by the crass humor which all of her associates in her television newsroom apply to the circumstances of Chuckle's death. She stalwartly maintains a disapproving attitude toward their behavior until she attends the funeral. There, while everyone else is finally showing some decorum, her Daimon plugs her in to the funny side.

During the eulogy, Mary begins to laugh uncontrollably. In this embarrassing fashion she discovers what her associates had seen all along: that, death notwithstanding, there was inherent humor in the specifics of Chuckles demise, a point in which a professional clown might well have taken some delight.

I feel good about the fact that my wife, Shirley, and I laughed quite a bit on the day before she lapsed into a coma and died. From that point we were never to have the opportunity to share words or laughter again.

On that last relatively good day of a terrible time we watched television together in her hospital room. In confirmation of Norman Cousin's assertions, she became unmindful of her considerable discomfort while we kept up the humor.

I remember that we watched the Early Movie on the tube. It happened to be possibly one of the worst films ever made. It was called The Black Shield of Falworth (Universal Pictures, 1954) and was about a nobleman, played by Tony Curtis, working his way through the stages leading to knighthood in medieval England.

We started having fun with the movie by being critical of everything about it. Curtis' acting was incredibly bad. We were hyperconscious of the fact that his real name is Bernie Schwartz as he went about uttering high toned English phrases in his native Bronx Jewish dialect. The film probably isn't as funny as we made it out to be but the laughter we enjoyed was a great tension reliever and left us with a relaxed, close feeling for the remainder of what was to be our last afternoon together.

Whenever I hear anything about The Black Shield of Falworth (which isn't very often) I undergo a rush of mixed feelings. There's a touch of sadness but it's laced with a real warm regard for that movie. My realization is, that of all the motion pictures in the world, it was the perfect one for Shirley and me on that particular day.

God bless Tony and the gang. And thank God for the Daimon who is willing and able to bring us healing gifts. If we let him lead us at times of crisis, chances are he will help us find some gently humorous aspect of the situation to aid us in seeing it through.

CHAPTER TEN

The Creative Gift

God saw all he had made, and indeed it was very good.

- The Book of Genesis
- The Jerusalem Bible

Next among the Daimon's gifts is enhancement of the human attribute we call creativity. Like healing, the creative experience is often associated with an altered state of consciousness.

Creation holds an honored place in all mythologies. Upon reading the account of the beginning of things in Genesis, we find God repeatedly judging his creations to be "good." Yaveh confirms that the work of creation is good work - God work. He generously allows human beings to share in this God work by making creativity a human attribute.

Our personal creativity elevates our stature among the inhabitants of the earth. Being creative is one of the ways in which we are allowed to enter into the province of the Divine.

In the pantheon of Ancient Greece, Apollo the Sun God was the greatest of the deities after Zeus. He was, among other things, the God of prophecy, poetry, music, medicine, oracles, healing, reason, inspiration, magic, divination, and the arts. Among his companions were the nine Muses, each excelling in a specific art or realm of knowledge. When mortal Greeks engaged in creative endeavors, they frequently identified their inspirational experiences as visits from one of the muses. In other words, they experienced their creative acts as having supernatural origin. This idea has not passed away.

Most who make the Daimonic connection notice a surge of creative energy after they embark on the quest for the Gleam. This is another of the Daimon's gifts.

Creative abilities are present in everyone to start with, so the Daimon is not the source of creativity but is the facilitator of it. You might say he, like Apollo, loves to dally with the Muses.

The Mystery Of Creativity

While we may do many creative things out of our own volition, at one time or another most of us have experienced the sensation of being inspired. The state of inspiration is an altered state of consciousness. The very origin of the word gives recognition to this.

"Inspiration" has its root in the Latin noun "spiritus" and is derived directly from the verb "inspiratio" which means to breathe in. Etymologically, "inspiration" describes a spirit breathed into an individual and infusing her with divine gifts.

Many creative people have described inspiration as the sensation of being influenced or invaded by what feels like an outside source. Through a mystical process this source imparts an original idea, an invention, a solution to a problem, or a complete work of art to its host. Those who have had the experience find it undeniable though quite inexplicable.

A characteristic of such events is that the Muse does not announce her arrival. She does not knock before entering. Suddenly, she is upon us and our creative cauldron is boiling.

Intuition, often identified as a parapsychological phenomenon, operates in a similar manner. An intuitive idea or awareness comes to us through a channel that is outside of our usual conscious, rational processing. In an instant we feel strongly or just "know" that a certain event is going to occur or has occurred or that a particular decision is the right or wrong one to make.

Both intuition and creativity are every day miracles that the Daimon actively accesses on our behalf. When the Daimon is suppressed or cast into the Shadow realm, our connection with our intuitive/creative function is diminished.

There are individuals who believe they have no creative ability at all. To some extent contemporary culture supports this notion by equating creativity with extraordinary talent in one or more of the arts. It goes without saying that most of us are not sufficiently endowed to contribute at this level.

Creativity has a more down-to-earth meaning that relates to originality and innovation. In this sense every one can be creative. We all have a capacity for original thinking and for looking at existing things in new or different ways.

The creative skills involved in writing, painting, composing and playing music, or giving a theatrical performance get exceptional recognition because of the pleasure they bring to us. Unfortunately, we seldom show similar appreciation for the creative wonder that lies behind developing a new recipe, taking an untried approach to child discipline, building a bird house, or blazing a nature trail across unexplored terrain.

Muse Denial Sickness

We all know that we have the ability to resist the call of the Daimon. His consorts, the Muses, have an equally compelling call when they appear, yet they too can be denied. The consequence of doing so may be harmful.

Several years ago, my client Bree discovered this. She was a young actress with a sparkling personality that could light up the stage in the dreariest of plays. She was also an only child whose parents were successful professionals in two different fields of science. For many years they and their daughter took it for granted that she would follow in one or the other of their footsteps.

They were proud of their over-achieving offspring and were understanding when she sought some diversion through the Drama Club in high school. Since she did all things well, they were not surprised that Bree turned in some excellent performances in the school plays. They didn't know that the magical atmosphere of the theater was awakening and energizing Bree's Daimon.

Before she graduated she had received and embraced the Muse. The parents were aghast when she announced her intention to major in drama at college. They did a considerable amount of ranting and raving, reminding her repeatedly that she would be breaking a family tradition going back several generations by not professing one of the sciences.

Bree was torn between "making her parents happy" and following the Gleam. She had discovered what was for her the primary source of enchantment and had no desire to give it up. She stuck by her decision even as her mother delivered increasingly ominous warnings that she was about to enter a world populated with perverts, phonies, exploiters, and substance abusers. The woman predicted that her daughter could not and would not remain unscathed in such an environment.

Besieged by guilt for being selfish, Bree managed to live up to her parents' expectations by sabotaging herself. In spite of quality academic work, by the time she graduated from college she had become involved in an abusive lesbian relationship and could not function without mood elevating drugs.

She returned home and accepted the need for a period of inpatient psychiatric treatment. During that time, she decided that her parents had known what was best for her all along. Soon after discharge, thinking her life was back in order, she entered graduate school as a sociology major.

Bree adopted a new lifestyle that was solidly conventional. She attended classes, studied diligently, socialized moderately, and established a steady relationship with a fellow student who was male.

After six months of this "good life," she became significantly depressed again. This time she did not resume her reliance on medication. Through referral from a friend she came to me for psychotherapy.

In our initial explorations everything pointed to my client's lack of fulfillment in her newly chosen, parentally sanctioned vocation as a central problem. When I confronted her with this she reacted with overwrought defensiveness.

Pounding the arm of her chair with her fist, Bree avowed she had no desire to be around actors. She described them as "vile people" and defined the stage as a "platform for the vanity and arrogance of perverse egomaniacs." She quoted unfounded statistics such as "ninety per cent of all theater people are queers, druggies, or both."

I allowed her to rave on until she ran out of steam. Then, I just looked at her.

When her eyes met mine, she blushed, embarrassed by her irrational tirade. "All right," she confessed with a sheepish smile, "I'm protesting too much. The truth is I love the theater. Acting uplifts me so much that I have to say it's a spiritual thing. I don't know any other way to experience that high. I don't even want to know another way."

We sat in silence for a moment and I watched her eyes fill with tears. She sighed heavily. "But on my way to Broadway I sure managed to make one hell of a mess of my life."

"And you've been blaming that on the lousy profession and the kooky people in it," I observed.

"Yes," she acknowledged. "I sound like a recording of my mother. I really know better. I made the mess on my own. I behaved immaturely and made some really bad choices."

From that point Bree and I were able to address her deep-seated guilt about disappointing and defying her parents. The debacle she created at college was her way of unconsciously punishing herself for going against them. She did this by proving them right.

We agreed that she needed to develop more self- discipline, no matter what her vocation. She made a commitment to continue to be selective about whom she chose for close relationships and to remain free from chemical dependence of any kind.

With this more mature and responsible attitude, she took her first step toward returning to the theater by securing a role in a community playhouse production. Life was breathed back into her Daimon who helped her give an "inspired" performance. Amid accolades, her confidence returned and her star, once again, began to ascend.

The old guilt instilling voices in her head did not immediately become silent. She developed the ability to talk back to them. She abetted her conflict with them by getting input from directors, colleagues, and audiences regarding her work.

It wasn't long before she took steps to change her graduate program to dramatic arts. Her parents distanced themselves from her again but, this time, with a little less vehemence. Her boyfriend split with her on the grounds that he didn't like having to share her with other actors and the public.

For the first time, none of this mattered much to Bree. She knew she was on the right path for her and felt fulfilled. She was following the Gleam.

Today this client is associated with a repertory company. She is oriented to career rather than marriage, and has many friends, one of whom is an occasional lover. She has appeared in some national television productions and hopes to eventually land a movie role or a part on Broadway. She does not use alcohol or drugs and maintains that their effect can't compare with the rush of being on stage in front of an appreciative audience.

With our Daimon confined to chambers, we may, like Bree, discount or deny our creative urges. With the Daimon freed it is not so easy to do so even if our external environment and others in our life are not supportive.

The Muse In Action

Given her tendency to appear without warning at any time of the day or night, the Muse is almost sure to be noticed. Some pretty well known people have given accounts of their visits with her. They credit her with bringing them information and imagery from a vast repository of forms and wisdom which lies beyond what can be accessed through ordinary, individual experience.

The chemist Kekule's dream of the benzene ring is an often-cited case in point as is Einstein's image of riding on a beam of light. By these scientists' own accounts, both of these revelations came from a source other than their rational conscious minds.

Rudyard Kipling wrote of listening to his "Personal Daemon;" Robert Louis Stevenson created stories with the assistance of dream helpers whom he called his "brownies;" Elias Howe solved the problem preventing perfection of his sewing machine with information transmitted in a dream; Percy Shelley declared that he and other poets receive their creations from somewhere beyond ordinary consciousness; Renee Descartes attributed the origin of his world changing philosophy of science to a series of dreams; and what school child is not familiar with Archimedes' "Eureka!" experience while languishing in his bathtub? There are volumes filled with accounts of visitations from the Muse. The creative moment is mysterious and often electrifying.

As a writer, I can attest to occurrences that confirm reports of the Muse's intervention. I have produced written works and parts of works that abruptly entered into my consciousness and seemed to have nothing to do with an act of will on my part. Granted, these represent only a fraction of my total output but I find them astonishing. By way of example, I am including here a piece of work generated by one of these curious incidents.

The product is a poem that seemed to come from some mystical source outside of myself. It is not great poetry but the way I came upon it exemplifies how extraordinary a creative act can be. Though it is compatible with my style of writing, I truly do not feel that I am the author of it.

I received the poem on a fall afternoon when I was at home alone and slightly bored. I was seated on the sofa thumbing through a catalog when I suddenly began having auditory images of words being chanted in tempo with a very simple musical schema. After listening to the entire piece and finding I could not get it out of my head, I went to my study and wrote down the words. Only after I had committed the poem to paper was I able to stop reciting it mentally.

Though the piece undoubtedly could be improved upon with additional work, I have chosen not to make any changes in the original dictation. I cherish the poem as beautiful thoughts sent to me from someone, somewhere.

> When the Buddha bells ring eventide,
> I'll be on the homeward track.
> When I stand along the Great Divide,
> There will be no looking back.
> For the lessons taught me, thanks, my lord,
> For the blindness I now see,
> For the way my mind and spirit soared
> When I glimpsed eternity.
> Good-bye solemn temples made of gold.

Good-bye lanterns in the night.
Good-bye little maidens, wise men old.
I am guided by your light.
Through the fiery sunset I shall walk,
Turn to ashes and arise,
Then, to climb the tallest flower stalk
And play with the butterflies.
When the Buddha bells ring eventide,
Let there be no missing me.
I am here forever at your side
In the mountains and the sea.

Perhaps this rhyme was transmitted telepathically. I don't know.

The phenomenon is similar to channeling with one exception. Most channeled information comes to its receiver from a source that identifies itself or is in some way identifiable. You will recall that the prophet Mohammed received the Islamic scriptures from a source that revealed itself to be the Angel Gabriel. Jane Roberts' books were dictated to her by an entity called Seth, and William Butler Yeats based his book, A Vision, on messages channeled from his deceased wife.

My experience, along with similar ones reported by such luminaries as the poet Rilke and the composer Mozart, has no specific source. This type of encounter with the Muse is perhaps most meaningfully described as spontaneous creativity. My Daimon, of course, does not attach much importance to classifying creative experiences. To him, they are simply elements of the shower of miracles that rains down on us every day.

Creativity and Self Actualization

Abraham Maslow (1954) contributed much to the field of psychology including the term "self-actualization." It is the concept of being all that we can be, utilizing our talents and abilities in the way that best expresses who we are.

Early in his studies, Maslow sought out persons whose talents had made them famous. He expected to be able to use them as examples of what a self-actualized person is like.

In the course of time he discovered that there were many talented and famous people who were not self- actualized. Others who were self-actualized could lay no claim to exceptional creative abilities.

This led Maslow to redefine creativity as not just a productive endeavor but a special way of living. He came to the viewpoint that self-actualized individuals are those who create and grow within the boundaries of their existence, no matter what their calling or social status.

Maslow's ultimate assessment supports the position that the Daimon is alive, well, and active in those who are self- actualized. His findings state that self-actualized persons make their day to day living an esthetic experience by facing with excitement the unknown, accepting themselves and others, being unpretentious, maintaining spontaneity, and holding their commitment to whatever life tasks they perceive to be their own. They are interested and interesting people, whether digging in a backyard garden or delivering a lecture from the podium.

Thus, creativity is no less a determinant of a great life than of great art. The creative living of life fully involves the body, mind, and spirit. The end result reveals the creator's soul just as readily as do works of art.

In life our choices are not infinite. It is the way we exercise the choices that we do have and what we make of their consequences that puts the stamp of our individual creativity on our lives.

Running Amuck With The Muse

Creativity is a god-like attribute but we are not gods. In each of us lie the seeds of hate, envy, prejudice, and destructiveness. No matter how well controlled, the force of evil dwells within every human being.

Some of us accept and maintain awareness of this part of ourselves as we seek to direct our energies toward those thoughts, feelings, and behaviors that promote growth and enrich our lives.

There are others who deny the destructive elements of their personality, convincing themselves that they could not possibly have such base emotions or motives.

Most of us live somewhere between the extremes of totally acknowledging our capacity for evil and totally denying it. To the extent it is denied, it is relegated to the Unconscious - put out of our awareness. There, it functions like a shadow. It is not me but it follows me around wherever I go.

In 1865, Robert Louis Stevenson (1966) published the poem, "My Shadow" in which, through innocent childish eyes, he contemplates this Other who follows him everywhere and wonders of what use he can be. A year later with the publication of <u>The Strange Case of Dr. Jekyll and Mr. Hyde</u>, Stevenson (1981), revealed to the world the nature of the Shadow side of the human personality in the character called Hyde, a primal creature bent on self fulfillment in defiance of moral and social codes. Hyde was the "not me" which Jekyll originally had relegated to his Unconscious but later gained ascendancy when the doctor carried out an ill begotten experiment. The evil Hyde, it turns out, was actually the stronger side of Jekyll's dual nature.

This story's continuing popularity right up to the present attests to the respondent chord it strikes in all of us. While most of us do not give ourselves over to this evil side as did Dr. Jekyll, we have an ongoing sense of its presence and recognize its power to influence to a greater or lesser degree what we do. This faces us with the necessity of being aware that our creative endeavors are not automatically immune to its influence.

It is possible to be creative with conscious or unconscious intent to encourage hatred, violence, lawlessness, or other destructive goals. The average citizen does not have to live very long before encountering pictures and written or spoken words dedicated to these ends. Is anyone unaware of contemporary musical forms that celebrate killing police, taking drugs, and abusing women?

On another level, consider all the creative work that has gone into the production of the hydrogen bomb, germ warfare, super destructive weaponry and other death dealing devices. Our entire culture was shocked when it was reported that two Colorado teenagers spent over a year creatively devising a plan to destroy Columbine High School and their fellow students. The creative execution of evil deeds reached its epitome with the despicable but ingeniously conceived terrorist attack on September 11, 2001, that threw our nation into such turmoil that we shall be engaged in reaction and recovery for years.

Created things are not of themselves innately good or bad. The capacity for working evil with things lies within those who read them, view them, hear them, buy them, or use them.

In addition to things created with evil intent, the creative process itself that can have a dark side. This is most apparent when creativity becomes an obsession.

While it is true that some of the best known creative minds like the Curies, Thomas Edison, and Albert Einstein have exhibited obsessive traits, there is a line beyond which creative work becomes a symptom of neurosis. People have been known to become so feverishly consumed with creativity that they have neglected hygiene, lost interest in food, completely withdrawn from social intercourse, and even gone mad.

It must also be noted that creative work may be based primarily on rivalry and competitiveness. This does not necessarily negate the value of the product but it is likely to limit the fulfilling or self-actualizing benefits for the creator. When motivated by the need to prove superiority or to reduce the stature of another, creativity is lowered to the level of a psychological defense mechanism.

Something In Return

Most everyone visited by the Muse feels privileged and grateful. At the very least, in return they reflect a reverence for this mystical force.

I know one person who has a special way of showing his appreciation. He is one of the many artists, writers, musicians, actors, and craftsmen who inhabit the community in which I am fortunate enough to live. I shall refer to him here as Harry.

Harry is a painter who is well connected to his vigorous Daimon. His artistic style is so in demand commercially that he sells his paintings almost as fast as he can produce them. He feels good about his works and the income they produce.

Harry also creates what he calls his "real art." These works come about through a felt involvement with the Muse, whereas his commercial paintings do not. I have seen a couple of the "real" ones and consider them to be extraordinary though they may not have widespread appeal.

He has confided to me that once or twice a year he becomes afflicted with an oppressive "aura" which will not lift until he does one of these special paintings. While engaged in creating them, he has the feeling that his hand is being completely guided by an unseen force and the work is completed in a very short time.

Harry has made it his practice to give these paintings away, being very selective regarding the recipients. Most have gone to family members. The quality of his productions certainly could command a substantial purchase price but he says giving them away is his method of showing appreciation to whomever or whatever (Harry is a spiritual person though not religious) guides his hand.

"After all," he says, "the painting was a gift to me in the first place."

CHAPTER ELEVEN

The Spiritual Gift

> If a star were confined into a tomb,
>   Her captive flames must needs burn there;
> But when the hand that locked her up gives room,
>   She'll shine through all the sphere.

> - Henry Vaughn
> "They Are All Gone…"

The Daimon seeks to free the Soul. When released by Ego, she becomes a wayfarer and a guide to the Soul. She constantly beckons us to follow her on expeditions of discovery that ultimately contribute to growth of the Soul. This guiding principle is the Daimon's spiritual gift to us.

"Follow me to follow the Gleam," she says and the Soul responds joyfully while the rational Ego hesitates. Just where and how far does she intend to take us?

As guardian of our entire being, the Daimon's primary function is to lead us to wholeness, ultimately holiness. We have already observed her engaged in such activities as healing the mind/body system, imparting wisdom, facilitating creativity, directing through intuition, revealing the Shadow side of personality, and exploring the farthest reaches of inner space.

These are all examples of the Spirit working in the service of flesh and psyche. Ego can grasp the advantages of this and give consent without too much discomfort but the Daimon (Spirit) has a special liaison with the Soul that Ego finds more alarming.

The Gleam hovers beyond the material universe. The Daimon's gift of spirituality offers the Soul an opportunity to transcend the physical world.

In ages past the veil between the material and non-material worlds was thinner. On any given day an ordinary citizen might encounter in a totally believable fashion some supernatural being or occurrence.

The incident might involve gods, devils, ghosts, angels, prophecies, revelations, heaven, or hell. When discussed at the dinner table, these visions would be accepted by others as completely credible.

In this modern age, we call such phenomena hallucinations, psychosis, drug trips, superstitions, or outright lies. The sophisticated Ego rejects the accessibility of, if not the existence of, a non-material realm. In the context of contemporary religious tenets we may talk about an afterlife and supernatural beings but it is usually an intellectualized reference to something that we believe cannot and maybe should not be directly experienced this side of death.

This prejudice notwithstanding, there are daily accounts of the barriers between the two worlds collapsing. Over the past thirty years, a majority of my psychotherapy clients have reported having had one or more encounters with something they considered to be supernatural. I suspect this would be the case in the broader population as well.

Interestingly, most of those reporting made no effort to repeat their paranormal experience. Many felt embarrassed by it. They rarely discussed the matter out of fear of being ridiculed or labeled "crazy." They felt concern that giving free rein to enthusiasm for such spiritual antics would lead to a desire for endless repetitions.

That assumption is not without foundation. Most of us have a deep yearning and insatiable curiosity that spurs us to discover the non-material world. It comes from the part of us we call Soul and the Daimon has a special responsibility to nurture and lead the Soul.

What The Soul Wants

In its attention to the Soul, the Daimon calls us to travel far, beyond the known and familiar, to the realm of no-thing-ness. This is the home of the Soul.

Twenty-first Century human beings tend to give little thought to the Soul, much less to its needs. Making the Daimonic connection restores a focus on the Soul and establishes a response mechanism to what it seeks.

What the Soul seeks first is recognition. No less than any other part of what composes our personhood, the Soul wants Ego to acknowledge its place in the self-system. It wants our consciousness to be aware of its existence and its desires.

Given recognition, the Soul next wants to participate in the thinking, feeling, and acting behaviors of the self-system. It wants to be part of the motivational force which moves us. It wants to have a voice in decision making. It wants Ego to turn over to it an allotment of time and energy.

The Soul's next need is for community. It wants some channel or channels for connecting with other Souls. This need may be met to a greater or less extent by organized religion but a spiritual partner, mentor, or group outside of the institutional church may serve as well.

The Soul also wants to have avenues enabling it to reach, explore, and spend time in the non-material universe. Some of the modalities for doing this will be described below.

Finally, the Soul seeks an experience of the Divine. The Soul strives to make contact (be in communion with) God by whatever name he/she is known (the supreme being, higher power, the source, etc.)

Assigned to nurture the Soul, the Daimon helps in every way possible to meet these needs to the extent that she is free to do so. Personal inhibitions, defenses, beliefs, fears, and socio-cultural prohibitions are agencies that limit her.

The Daimon abets the effort to transcend by facilitating a search for transcendent methodology. As we discuss a few of the many possible methods, you will recognize that all of them have been woven into the world's major spiritual disciplines to some extent and receive special emphasis in the mystical traditions embedded in those disciplines.

The methods we shall note here are:
1. Ordeals and the Use of Psychoactive Substances
2. The Observance of Silence
3. Meditation
4. Prayer
5. Imagery

The Shamanic Way

The way of the shaman is probably the oldest of humankind's mystical paths. Ordeals and the use of mind altering drugs are deeply rooted in this tradition.

In so-called primitive cultures the shaman was a man or woman endowed with special gifts enabling him or her to be transported to the spirit world. This was accomplished by entering a spontaneous or induced altered states of consciousness.

While in the spirit world the shaman might obtain needed information, find a lost soul, do battle with evil spirits, negotiate forgiveness with the gods, or cut a deal with them for some desired blessing. Along with wisdom, cures, prophecies, or advice for individuals and the entire tribe, the shaman would return from his journey with stories and songs about the landscape and various entities encountered in the spirit world.

It was commonplace for acts of mortification or a self- imposed ordeal to precede the shaman's embarkation to the spirit world. Fasting, sleep deprivation, exposure to the elements, isolation in the wilderness, and the infliction of pain were common ritualized procedures. Anyone caring to test these procedures will find them just as effective today as generators of a visionary experience.

It should not be overlooked that ancient shamans possessed considerable knowledge about the mind-altering qualities of certain plants and herbs. They were often used in ritualistic functions. They also made use of drum banging, chanting, and marathon dancing as means of entering into a trance state.

The shamanic techniques for transcendence are so effective that they have been incorporated into culture after culture throughout history. The vision quest of the Native Americans, the wilderness wanderings of the Christian saints, and the acid dropping of the hippies in the 1960's are all reflections of this tradition.

Given the legal restrictions on the use of psychedelic drugs I shall not here place special emphasis on their relative value in inducing transcendent experiences. I think it only fair to say, however, that despite the large numbers of persons who use such drugs recreationally or addictively, there are those who maintain a serious and legitimate interest in the use of mind altering substances to initiate or enhance travel in the spirit world or to investigate their potential for mind expansion. Until and if such use of these substances is authorized there are other effective, safe, and legal pathways which can be explored.

Ordeals at varying levels of pain and risk continue to offer magical possibilities. If you are physically able and your Daimon beckons you to pursue this course, there are rewards to be reaped.

Ordeals do not have to be structured on the scale of the Sun Dance or a hike across the Sahara. With a little imagination you can fashion one which is in keeping with your fitness level and your social surroundings.

The Painless Quest of Sophie Greene

One of my clients, a homemaker whom we shall call Sophie, was prompted by her Daimon to make a spiritual quest. She was a somewhat pampered woman, not inclined toward, nor in good shape for, a journey in the wilderness. So, quite creatively she planned a sojourn that would not take her more than a few miles from her home.

Sophie resolved to leave her house on foot in the morning and to remain away until sundown. Her plan was to spend the day as a wanderer, allowing birds, other animals, and plant life to draw her in this direction or that while abstaining from food and drink and avoiding commercial establishments.

One of the highlights of Sophie's quest occurred when she sought a cool place to rest at mid-morning. She found a vacant lot carpeted with pine needles fallen from the tall trees that all but blotted out the sun. Entering the cool and quiet wooded area, she immediately felt she had discovered a sacred place.

Sitting with her back against a tree trunk, Sophie closed her eyes and listened to the music of the Gulf breezes rustling the pines. After a brief period of reverie, an attention demanding staccato filled her ears. Looking toward its source, she glimpsed the imposing figure of a pileated woodpecker. The red on its head lent color to its rapid-fire pecking motions as it beat out a series of rhythmic tattoos with its beak.

She was privileged to watch the bird go about its work for several minutes. During this time the thought came to her that the bird may have been sent to teach her something. The intensity of its drilling conveyed to her that it was "digging hard and deep," perhaps modeling something for her.

Upon reflection, Sophie connected the woodpecker's behavior with her heretofore unsuccessful efforts to discover new dimensions of herself. She realized she does not drive herself hard enough to expand the horizons of her awareness. She concluded that she needed to dig deeper in her therapeutic work.

By the evening of her quest day, Sophie was sweat soaked, thirsty, and footsore but exhilarated by the several enlightening observations she had been able to make during her hike. That night, her husband took her to a restaurant where she ate heartily and joyfully shared her new insights with him.

Later in my office, smiling with satisfaction, she told of her meeting with the bird and declared that its most obvious message was that she needed to use her head more. She needed to be more intense and diligent in the pursuit of her goals and to analyze herself more deeply. It was advice she took to heart.

Since the publication of The Way of the Shaman by Michael Harner (1982) and other works on the subject, there has been a resurgence of interest in shamanic practices in the United States. Harner has established the Foundation of Shamanic Studies which offers training courses in shamanic techniques as well as dissemination of educational materials for those who want to deepen their knowledge of this method of transcendence.

The Splendor of Silence

One of the under-emphasized tools for transcendence is the observance of silence. The centrality of silence is implied in the choice some make to withdraw to caves or the wilderness in order to make contact with the non-material world. More formally, silence has a well established place in the Christian tradition wherein silent prayer is frequently advocated and silence is observed during religious retreats. In monastic life daily periods of silence are often the rule and in some orders a scared vow is made to observe silence as a way of life.

In North American culture there is little tolerance for silence. Clients new to therapy, especially group therapy, become visibly anxious when protracted moments of silence for reflection occur during a group session. Of course, many therapists have the same response.

Our culture places little value on silence and, in fact, quiet individuals are apt to be perceived as dull, stuck up, or socially inept. The Western ideal is the dynamic person who articulates loudly and clearly while working and playing aggressively. Those who are less verbal may unjustly be labeled dull, passive, or passionless.

Yet, even the most casual observer cannot avoid recognizing that the healing value of silence historically has been a cornerstone of medical practice. For generations physicians have advised patients suffering from significant injury or disease to "rest and stay quiet." It is a given that periods of silence restore and revitalize the mind/body system.

It is in periods of silence that we can most clearly hear what the Soul has to say. If we want connection with her we must get beyond that point on the inner journey where we are in contact with the incessant dialogue going on between the various subselves of our personality. That is a useful level for therapeutic work but not necessarily for listening to the Soul.

Beyond the inner realm of unceasing chatter there is one of stillness which, when entered upon, may produce feelings similar to those experienced when we sense that we are standing on holy ground or have in some other way entered into the presence of the Divine. It is here that we enter the Kingdom Within of which Jesus spoke. It is a section of inner space similar to a chapel or grotto wherein one senses an immediate communion with a higher power.

Bernadette Roberts (1982) who was a cloistered nun for ten years writes about her experience with various types of silence in her book entitled, The Experience of No-Self. She reports becoming aware early in her childhood of the peaceful silence that accompanies feeling at one with the environment, an experience many of us may have shared.

At a later stage, Roberts was able to silence her mind, disengaging from all the business being transacted there and drifting into the depths of darkness. Then in her teens she discovered an even more profound silence which she recognized as the silence at the inner core of her being. She identified this silence as the constant, immutable center of her Self and ultimately came to identify it as God.

Simplistic as it may sound, entering into silence, being receptive to what can be heard beyond our noisy minds is a highway to transcendence. Our self-orientation is manifest in our incessant need to express ourselves and in our preoccupation with what our inner voices have to say. In silence we let go of this and escape the boundaries of humanity.

The Meditative Way

In practice there are many different forms of meditation. All have a transcendent function.

One form calls upon us to focus our complete attention on some object, sound, image, or task. Frequently chosen objects of visual focus are a crucifix, a holy picture, a candle flame, or a mandala. Sounds chosen include mantras and phrases from sacred literature. In addition, an infinite number of mental images are available. Concentration on breathing or energy centers of the body such as the sixth chakra (located between the eyes) may be used. Whatever the focus, the intention is to become totally immersed in the object, sound, image, or function.

In another form of meditation, the subject seeks to eliminate all images and dialogues from his mind. The goal here is to experience nothingness (no-thing-ness) which is the fertile ground from which all that is arises.

All meditative practices have in common the effect of quieting the mind. The quieted mind opens up to us the "something more" which exists in all things physical. The next step is to dissolve the boundaries between that mystical realm and ourselves, thereby becoming one with it.

This process has the potential to bring us to what some call enlightenment. It has been realized by only a few great souls during their earthly tenure but, short of attaining the permanently enlightened state, there remain many benefits to be accrued from meditation through its transcendent, healing, relaxing, and mind clearing functions.

Meditative methods have been devised and prescribed by all of the world's great religions. Some place emphasis on assuming certain postures, some provide the practitioners with particular mantras, mandalas, or prayer forms. Some insist on a rigorous schedule of meditation and others promote it as an optional activity, but most noteworthy is the fact that all see value in the practice of it.

The Prayerful Way

Prayer is another vehicle for transcendence when its goal is to contemplate or commune with the Divine. More often prayer is used to ask for something for one's self or others. Thanksgiving and confession are other frequent themes of prayer.

In prayers of supplication, the Higher Power is asked to provide the petitioner with what he needs spiritually and/or materially. Sometimes the request is made on behalf of another. The Lord's Prayer, reputedly composed by Jesus, embodies most of these types of prayer, combining words of praise with requests for spiritual nourishment, protection from Evil, and forgiveness of self and others.

Transcendent prayer is directed toward transporting one's self to the realm of the Divine. The early Christian mystics made much of Christ's declaration that the Kingdom of God is within. Taking the statement literally they placed emphasis on knowing God through prayer, meditation, mortification, and withdrawal from the world. This approach was predicated on the belief that through a very personal process the Divine could be discovered by each individual in his or her inner world.

St. Teresa of Avila (1980) and other Christian mystics achieved states of ecstasy through forms of prayer which were not discursive. In her writings, Teresa described what she called prayer of reconciliation, which is conducted silently in a state of vigilant receptivity to the influx of spirit. It is a method of achieving self-dissolution and unity with God.

Teresa's spiritual practices got her censured by the Church. Her spiritual colleague, St. John of the Cross, was sent to prison for a time. Reaching ever higher levels of organization, the institutional church was moving away from acceptance of personal mysticism. The clergy was appointed to be the interpreting and determining body regarding the correct experience of God. An individual's personal experience of the Divine was considered inferior to the teachings of the Church and, if regarded as heretical, could be severely punished.

In the modern world, institutionalized religious bodies still tend to prescribe the form and content of prayer that they deem to be appropriate for their people. Devout Moslems are required to pray five times daily facing Mecca no matter where they may be. The orthodox Hindu incorporates religious ritual into almost every act of daily life and recites mantras (sounds embodying a particular deity's power) many times over.

In Judaism there is a long-standing tradition of conversational prayer dating back to Abraham and Moses. Those of us who saw the stage or movie version of <u>Fiddler on the Roof</u> will recall with delight this prayer form being reflected in the milkman Tevye's little talks with God in which he tells his creator exactly how he feels about things, including his complaints.

In the Christian churches of today some of the formality relating to prayer has been relaxed. Prayers in Latin are no longer a requirement in the Roman Catholic Mass (although in some areas they are being utilized by popular demand) and the Episcopal Church allows prayer in the modern idiom as well as King James' English.

In some faiths people are taught to kneel to pray. In others, they stand, sit, or prostrate themselves. Likewise, some denominations stress reading prayers from a book while others encourage extemporaneous prayer. Some favor praying aloud, while others pray silently.

The Daimon may not attach much importance to the postures or protocols of prayer. He is eager to put us in communication with God at any time, any place, and under any circumstances.

Many individuals have reported that while at prayer they sense the presence of God more keenly. Using prayer to attain that feeling of greater intimacy with the Almighty is both legitimate and rewarding.

One can combine meditative and prayerful modalities in an effort to establish communication with the Divine. In fact, this approach can lead to powerful encounters with the entire spiritual landscape, an experience that can be both exalting and frightening.

At The Gate Of The Kingdom

When a gentleman named Josh entered therapy seeking to recapture his lost sense of wonder, he didn't know it would lead him to the gate of the Kingdom Within. One of the first questions I asked was whether he could recall any time in his life when each new day brought to his awareness something which elicited his wonder or amazement.

Immediately Josh was taken back to his childhood days, many of which seemed full of enchantment. Now, as he approached mid-life, he recognized it had been many years since he'd been in touch with that childhood world which he called "make believe."

When we discussed the possibility of calling forth his Daimon to restore his sense of wonder, Josh was ambivalent. He was still conservatively committed to the religion in which he was raised and didn't care much for my emphasis on imagination and psychic forces. At the same time, he confessed that he was finding his religious practice increasingly rote and uninvolving.

I suggested that his Daimon would probably be delighted to help him breathe some fresh air into his spiritual practices. Josh cautiously agreed to image his long repressed Daimon and was presented with a marvelous metaphor. It was an Anglican bishop in his full regalia - mitre, crozier, and all - but wearing pink tinted designer glasses ala Elton John.

In dialogue with the bishop whose name was Fred, Josh confided that he prayed regularly but that his prayers no longer held any meaning for him. He stated that he read most of his prayers from The Book of Common Prayer, the Anglican prayer book which contains specific prayers for just about everything imaginable.

Fred suggested that Josh take a more innovative approach to prayer, assuring him that doing so would not violate his basic theology. They concluded he might benefit from overlaying a meditative model on his prayers.

With my assistance, Josh and Fred mapped out an approach with Josh agreeing to keep a record of its effect in a journal. Here is his account of his experiment.

"At my first session, I went through my relaxation procedure and attempted to put myself in a state of receptive openness. Right away, I encountered lots of clutter in my head. All sorts of irrelevant, trivial thoughts were suddenly vying for my attention. I continued to focus on my breathing and the static subsided somewhat but continued to plague me periodically throughout the session.

"Next, I began repeating the phrase, 'Come, Jesus.' I said the word 'come' when I inhaled and 'Jesus' when I exhaled. I continued for about fifteen minutes but was left with no feeling of having really prayed. I ended with no sense of having just done a spiritual exercise.

"I'm afraid this stuff is just not for me but will fulfill my commitment to experiment with it for the next few weeks."

As is often the case, things got worse for Josh before they got better. His seventh session went like this:

"Tonight as I began my meditation some hideous images began to appear in my mind's eye. They were contorted, disfigured faces apparently belonging to horribly deformed persons. They seemed to be laughing and sneering at me. It wasn't an auditory experience but I knew they were saying dirty things about me and telling me there is no God to hear my prayer.

"It was like being besieged by demons. They seemed very real. I had a sense of evil when they appeared. My body jerked and twisted despite my having initially reached a good level of relaxation. I found myself whispering 'Come, Jesus' more rapidly and loudly as their torment continued, forgetting about synchronizing the words with my breathing. I just wanted Jesus to come and chase all that evil away.

"The more I said it, though, the more vivid the faces became - and the more threatening. I began to think of them as real entities - bad spirits - intent on keeping me from my prayer.

"With great effort, I forced my eyes open. I could feel my heart pounding and my armpits were drenched. It took me several minutes to calm down.

"I spent some time thinking rationally about what had happened and how real it seemed. I felt a new found appreciation for people who believe there are devils roaming around out there. Only when I was fully collected could I confirm for myself that they were my own demonic images. I know they represent some kind of evil within myself.

"With my return to calmness I could not escape the realization that, while my experiments had brought me no closer to God, they had succeeded in bringing me face to face with some dark force. I was left with the conviction that there is more to this business than I had imagined.

"If this prayer form has the power to stir up so many demons inside of me, it may well have the power to bring me more into the presence of God. Whatever those images represent, I know they are from within and that I must find some way to deal with them. I am thoroughly frightened by the experience but am now completely determined to go on."

Fred had seen fit to lead Josh to the gates of hell en route to paradise. Subsequent therapy verified that the client truly did need to confront these elements of his Shadow side before he could be healed - made whole.

While we made this our focus in therapy, Josh continued his sessions of meditative prayer. On the next few tries, the demons continued to appear. On one occasion, battling with them made him nauseous and he had to flee to the bathroom to vomit. For a brief time he felt locked in a struggle for the life of his spirit. Perhaps he was.

To his credit, Josh kept up the fight in his therapy sessions and at home. The vile images from his Shadow side turned out to be representations of blasphemous ideas that he had entertained during a period in early adulthood when he was seriously studying and questioning scripture. His guilt about those "terrible ideas" had never been resolved.

At that time he had concluded that Jesus was a homosexual. Though these ideas were eventually put out of his consciousness, they had been what he called "damning thoughts." Fred's wearing those flamboyant pink glasses was a clue that he was going to help Josh confront all of this.

Repressing his sacrilegious thoughts had not prevented Josh from feeling that his connection with God was broken. To prevent any further breakthrough of the sacrilege, he invested great energy in sticking rigidly to the rubrics of the Church. Reading his prayers from the prayer book was one of the ways he guarded against being dangerously spontaneous. Having blocked out his original forbidden thoughts and his defenses against them, he had no way of understanding why his religious practices had become increasingly empty with the passage of time.

Josh's experiment ultimately helped him to reestablish his sense of being in communion with the Divine. One of his later journal entries reads as follows:

"I can see I've come a long way. Now, when I relax I have a kind of emptying sensation. It's like all of my emotional and physical insides are spilled out and what's left behind is a me I know very little about.

"When I get to that place, I sense there being lots of space around me and I say, 'Come, Jesus' with the expectation that Christ can and will fill that space and that we will be two in one space.

"This hasn't happened in any kind of complete way yet. There are moments of overwhelming sweetness when it seems about to, but it doesn't fully materialize. I know it will, though, because it can. I just have to create the right conditions and the Lord will respond.

"The sense of process is very exciting. Jesus is coming to me or vice-versa. We are moving closer. Something is happening. All the old boredom is gone."

Josh is reaching new heights of spirituality. At the same time, he is expanding awareness of himself. He is no longer waiting around, hoping that God will zap him with a little spiritual union. He is actively pursuing it. He is doing his part. He is, as he said, making it possible for God to respond.

The final mode of transcendence we shall explore is imagery. It is a technique of such power that it will occupy a chapter of its own. Read on.

CHAPTER TWELVE

Going Where No One Can Go

If thou be'st born to strange sights,
Things invisible to see,
Ride ten thousand days and nights,
Till age snow white hairs on thee;
Thou, when thou returns'st will tell me
All strange wonders that befell thee.

- John Donne
Song

Imagination allows us to break the bonds that shackle us to the material world. As stated early on, imagery is the language of things spiritual.

The non-material universe is accessible through intense, focused imagining that usually induces an altered state of consciousness. While another person's images are not directly observable, an altered state of consciousness is. When not operating in a normal state of consciousness, an individual manifests identifiable behaviors and changes in his/her brain waves patterns can be recorded in an electroencephalogram.

The effect of imagery on various physiological systems is also scientifically observable. The psychological impact of certain images can be validated by even an untrained observer when they produce intense emotions such as fear or joy.

Images can affect respiration, heart rhythms, blood pressure, and other physiological processes. They can also facilitate blood clotting and enhance the complicated chemistry of the immune system. In ways we don't fully understand, imagery has the power to influence various systems and even individual cells of our bodies.

However, our focus here is not on the physiological impact of this mysterious force called imagery. We are interested in how it revives and nurtures the Soul and expands the mind. As noted in Chapter One, the sacredness with which images were endowed and the magical power attributed to them has been recognizable at least since the creation of the ancient cave drawings and the shamanic practices connected with them.

The spiritual nature of imagery has been thematic in untold numbers of philosophies and religions. In our Judeo/Christian tradition, the Gospel of John provides us with a scriptural example of this theme. It opens with the statement, "In the beginning was the Word…"

Many people find this confusing because "Word" as used here is a poor translation of the Greek "logos." Logos has no English equivalent and encompasses in its meaning: thought, idea, and essence. So, John is saying, "In the beginning was the idea (image)." The idea to which he refers is the archetypal idea of one sent from God to lead humankind.

Through the sublime language of imagery the Daimon heals us and leads us toward our Soul's desire. Sometimes it is a gently evolving kind of healing and leadership that gradually increases inner peace and imparts a "knowing" which extends beyond believing. Sometimes Daimonic leadership is much more active as when generated by crisis, anguish, and despair unto death.

The Eleventh Hour Guide

The story of Calvin is an outstanding example of the transcendent function of the Daimon. It illustrates his ability to connect us with the Divine through imagery though we are in the throes of utter hopelessness.

The first thing this client said to me was that he had not come to me for help. He described himself as "beyond help." He did not believe he could benefit from psychotherapy and, even if he could, he didn't want to. He was consulting me solely to pacify his wife and some friends who were concerned about him.

He was quite open in his admission that two months prior to our meeting he had begun planning to kill himself. He wanted me to understand that his presence in my office did not mean he had changed his mind. All of this was said matter-of-factly and with little display of emotion, a chilling manifestation of his seriousness.

Cal acknowledged being deeply and cynically depressed but maintained that this was what life had taught him to be. It was obvious that he had been sorely wounded by life. He referred to it as "one big crucifixion," a term I found curious. I asked him why he used this particular metaphor.

His detailed explanation began with his identifying himself as the son of a Methodist minister. His father was unanimously adored by all in his congregation. His sermons were eloquent and mostly stressed salvation and the power of positive Christian values. The parishioners invariably left the church feeling uplifted. In the darkest moments of their lives the pastor's presence and prayers were their greatest consolation.

In the home, this right hand man of God displayed a different set of traits. He was strict, harsh, and demanding. He expected his wife and children to model every Christian virtue to the fullest in order to set an example for the families of the parish at all times.

Cal, the most outspoken of the pastor's three children, complained about the excessive restrictions imposed by his father. For such resistance, he was frequently punished by flailing with a broad black belt that his father called his "Jesus belt."

"Think of the crucifixion," Cal was told as the leather raised welts on his buttocks, "and you won't complain about your petty little hardships." The boy did think about it and it was his conclusion that Jesus had the better deal.

"He only got nailed once," Cal said pointedly, "but I was getting it two or three times a week."

At an early age Cal came to perceive his father and everything related to religion as hypocritical. He felt none of the love his father so generously radiated toward his sheep. He found no comfort in his father's personal interpretation of God's will.

By the time Calvin graduated from high school he was totally disillusioned. He knew nothing of giving or receiving tenderness and doubted that anyone enters into a relationship for any reason other than the exploitation of another.

In college this young man drank excessively and barely managed passing grades. Under the influence of alcohol he was involved in some mildly antisocial escapades which nearly got him suspended and brought embarrassment to his parents. No longer able to discipline his son with the Jesus belt, the father simply treated him with contempt.

In his sophomore year Cal got a girl pregnant and denied any responsibility. She ended up getting an abortion without his assistance.

In his senior year he met his wife-to-be. She was basically a loving person, albeit excessively willing to suffer in the name of love. She recognized Cal's inner pain and responded to it compassionately.

Idealistically she believed she could help him overcome his depression and negativism through the sheer power of her love for him. He liked her caring attitude enough to risk marriage but continued to doubt the depth of her commitment and her sincerity. He assumed she would eventually tire of him and leave.

By a lucky quirk of fate, as Cal perceived it, he secured a good job in the marketing field after graduation from college. From the beginning he wondered how long it would take his superiors to discover how inadequate he was.

To please his wife, Terri, he reluctantly agreed to their conceiving a child. He insisted that kids are nothing but trouble, while she argued that it would give him his first opportunity to be part of a loving family unit, an experience that would change his entire outlook. (She was ever optimistic.)

The baby was born with a heart defect. The new parents were plunged into a medical nightmare until corrective surgery could be performed. The first several months of parenthood left both Cal and Terri mentally and physically exhausted as well as heavily in debt.

Just as the baby's condition began to improve Cal lost his job, not because of incompetence, but because of corporate cutbacks. Unable to find another position in his field, he signed on as a furniture salesman at a much reduced income. He was soon hating to get up to go to work each morning.

These were the circumstances that prevailed at the time of his first appointment. He concluded his recitation of them by saying he had "one bit of good news."

It seems that a couple of days after he began seriously contemplating suicide, he discovered a lump about the size of a marble in his neck while shaving. He had been checking on it regularly and believed it to be increasing in size. His conclusion was that he had a cancerous growth and that, if he just let it go, his family could be spared the stigma of his committing suicide. In an effort to conceal the condition from everyone he had become more than usually withdrawn and it was this factor that had led Terri and others to insist on his seeing a therapist.

When Cal finished his story I told him that I took his intentions quite seriously and strongly recommended that he allow me to refer him for medication. He adamantly refused.

That being the case, I expressed the opinion that he was showing much wisdom in deciding to let the cancer run its course. While it would take a little longer, it would not deprive his family of much needed insurance benefits and would spare them some possible social repercussions. On this point, he verbalized agreement.

I went on to give recognition to the excellent use he had made of his intellect in reaching his decision. In truth there was much irrationality in his thinking but I wished to avoid taking an entirely oppositional stance which could close the door on doing any therapeutic work. No matter what motivated him consciously, he had come to see me, he was talking about his feelings, and he was not imminently suicidal by virtue of the real or imagined cancer which had taken him off the hook. (I wanted to build on all of that, if possible.)

I wondered out loud if his Unconscious endorsed his plan or perhaps had a better one. I suggested that out of a commitment to thoroughness he and I should spend a couple of sessions exploring that dimension of his psyche.

He glared at me through lusterless eyes, then spoke. "I slept through Psych. 101. I didn't then and still don't buy this idea of the Unconscious. Obviously you're trying to get me to change my mind and this is your strategy. It isn't going to work."

160

"Asking you to listen to a part of yourself is not exactly persuasion," I responded. "Your mind is making choices. I just want you to be sure you're using all of it. I don't think you are, but for all I know that part of you thinks you're right on track. Hopefully, we could check that out. As long as you want to give that knot on your neck a chance to develop and since you apparently care enough about Terri to have come to see me at her request, why not make use of what I have to offer?"

"And just what is that?" he asked skeptically.

"I can teach you how to get in touch with a part of yourself that can guide and inform you regarding what to do and how to do it. I want you to listen to that part of you, not to me. It's a personality component that has been with you all of your life but from the brief history you've given me, I'm sure you lost touch with it early in your development. Maybe sometimes it has spoken to you like a still, small voice in the night. Did you ever sense something like that?"

A wistful expression replaced Cal's sad countenance. "That sounds like what my mother used to call my Guardian Angel."

"Yes," I confirmed, "that's the name often given to it in the Christian tradition."

He quickly reverted to surliness. "Well, there's no such thing."

"Apparently it seemed real enough at one time," I challenged. "Maybe you're just put off by the link with a religious image. No matter what label was put on it, it is a function of your personality. I'm prepared to help you get acquainted with it at our next meeting. What do you say?"

My intuition said that Cal's commitment to self- destruction was not total. Some part of him seemed to be crying out for the "something more" which might justify going on with life. I viewed him as wanting help but needing a face-saving way to get it. I hoped I had offered him one.

For a moment he stared thoughtfully at the carpet. "I say this is bullshit," he announced, looking up, "but I'll come back to make Terri happy."

I breathed a sigh. I knew at the most I had bought a little time but in this case time meant opportunity to do some psychospiritual work. Had Cal refused further contact I should have found it necessary to take steps toward having him involuntarily hospitalized. I did inform him that ethics and fairness required my making Terri aware that he was suffering from depression, had been having suicidal thoughts, and should not be left alone. We agreed that it would not be necessary for him to tell her about his ace in the hole, the "cancer."

By way of a therapeutic footnote let me clarify that my handling of this client in no way suggests that I did not regard him as being seriously depressed and suicidal. Medication for symptom relief had been suggested and, of course, refused. Insistence on hospitalization could have been justified in the beginning but I knew it remained an option should outpatient therapy fail. My strongest sense was that Cal was in the middle of a spiritual emergency and that medication and/or hospitalization would leave this unresolved.

A couple of days later Cal returned and was willing to follow my suggestions for relaxing. His relaxation level was not deep but I forged ahead and asked him to travel in his imagination to a place of his own choosing where he would feel at peace with his surroundings.

He told me he was in a quiet cabin deep in the woods and I had him describe the scene in considerable detail. As he got increasingly involved in the description I could tell he had a sense of really being there.

Next, I asked him to step outside and find a comfortable spot to wait for his Guide (Daimon) to appear. I instructed him that Guides appear in a variety of forms, most often as living things but not necessarily human. I encouraged him to just wait patiently and alertly until something caught his attention and, then, to focus intently on whatever that might be.

Cal fell silent. Although I have learned to be patient during this procedure, the passage of time was excruciating in this instance. I knew that time was running out for Cal. My awareness that his life was literally at stake aroused anxiety in me that the technique might not work this time.

I reassured myself. "Of course it will work. I've seen it work over and again. There's no reason to think it won't work this time."

Minutes ticked by.

Finally, in the midst of what had become for me an oppressive silence, Cal suddenly let out a laugh of surprise.

It startled me. I jumped. "What are you in touch with?"

His voice conveyed a degree of excitement. "This is incredible," he said. "There's this little gray elephant trying to get in my lap. It's like something out of Disney. Well...actually it is. I recognize him. It's Dumbo...only it's not Dumbo. It's a little stuffed toy made in his likeness. It's familiar. It's a little Dumbo doll I had when I was - gosh, I don't know - I must have been only three or four. God, I loved that toy."

There was a pause. Cal sat there smiling, attentive to his image.

"It's my Dumbo doll...only he's like alive! He's jumping all around like he's glad to see me. I used to go to sleep holding him. I whispered into his big ears and told him I loved him. I think he was a gift from my favorite aunt. What a great old friend!"

Cal was obviously enjoying his image greatly.

"I'm sure this is your Guide," I said. "Thank him for coming."

Cal awkwardly verbalized thanks out loud. Even more awkwardly he followed my suggestion to enter into dialogue with his Guide.

Hurriedly, as if to get it over with, he asked the image if it had a name. He beamed with delight over the response he got.

"I'm Dumbo. Don't you remember? You used to take me everywhere you went."

A tear streamed down Cal's cheek. "Yes, I do remember. My parents didn't allow pets. I used to say you were my little puppy. I don't remember anything in my entire childhood being as warm and soft as you."

Tears were now rolling down his cheeks in profusion.

When asked where he had been all this time, Dumbo reported that he had remained Cal's favorite toy for several years and that, like the Skin Horse, he sort of got loved to pieces. He said Cal's mother had spirited him away one night because she saw that he was disintegrating.

Dumbo told of spending some sad days at the dump before being turned to ashes. He knew Cal was crying for him, so he came to him in some dreams to let him know they were bound together by love forever.

He was overwhelmed with joy over Cal's calling him back during this imagery session. He jumped into his beloved master's arms and licked his face, his "puppy" once again.

While communicating with his long lost friend Cal held his arms against his chest as if holding the little fellow. He wept and smiled at the same time.

When our hour had expired Cal found himself reluctant to leave his childhood pal. They parted with an agreement that they would meet again during our next therapy session, three days hence.

Upon returning to his ordinary state of consciousness Cal was incredulous. The experience had been so touching and so profound that there was no way he could discount it. Yet, its hopeful message of loving reconciliation was totally opposed to the negativism and pessimism characterizing his conscious thoughts.

At his next appointment Cal reported having felt "different" during the interim. He said he felt as if "some kind of spell" had been cast over him. He could not otherwise clarify his mental state.

Still unready to be positive, Cal began the session with an expression of doubt that Dumbo would appear again. He had been doing a considerable amount of worrying about that eventuality ever since we last met.

I asked if he really wanted to see Dumbo. When he replied in the affirmative I told him I had known many individuals to desert their Guides but not vice-versa. I expressed confidence in their meeting again.

When Dumbo appeared Cal visibly relaxed and shed more tears, which now seemed to be joyful. He cuddled and spoke to his spirit toy just as he had long ago.

Cal and I had previously agreed that, at this time, he would ask Dumbo's opinion about the suicide plan. After some general visiting, he did.

Dumbo immediately told him there was something he must see and, flapping his ears, became airborne. "Follow me," he said as he began to lead Cal up a mountainside.

Dumbo, in flight, stayed just ahead, offering Cal words of encouragement as he made the difficult, sometimes perilous climb.

Interestingly, from the beginning of the journey Cal did not show the slightest hesitation about letting the image guide him.

At last they reached the top and discovered there a stately white temple with massive columns. Dumbo directed Cal to go inside.

Immediately upon entering Cal had the feeling of being in a holy place. There was so much light in the temple that he was momentarily blinded. By shielding his eyes he was able to distinguish the form of a white-haired, bearded man in a long white robe. As the figure drew closer Cal noted that he had shining gray eyes and a penetrating gaze.

The man beckoned his visitor to follow and they entered into a large chamber adorned wall to wall with books. Standing in the center of the room the man raised his arms and gestured toward the hundreds of volumes surrounding them.

"I'm so glad to see you," he said, his voice deep and resonant. "I have tried many times to get your father here but he did not respond. I had fears that you would not either."

Cal's vision was clearing. "Where am I?" he asked.

"You're in the Place of Opportunity," he was told. "We have here what no one has ever taught you. We have the knowledge that you need and it is waiting for you to possess it.

"As long as you live, you may come here and learn as often as you like. When you die, this place will no longer be available to you."

"All these books," Cal said looking about, "is this what I need to know?"

The man nodded. "No one learns it all but each time you visit more and more of the wisdom here will be imparted to you, if you wish."

"There are so many," Cal said, awestruck, gazing at the books. "What are they about?"

The man smiled warmly, his gray eyes illuminated. "Love."

"You're right. I don't know anything about it," my client conceded.

"You know enough to get started," said the figure in white. "It was love that brought you here - little Dumbo. Love of anyone or anything is never trivial. It's what makes life worth living."

Cal's eyes popped open as if he had been catapulted back into the here and now. There were beads of sweat on his forehead and upper lip.

"This is too preposterous to be false," he said agitatedly. "It isn't even the kind of thing I would make up. It's utterly real. A moment ago I was in that temple."

Since then, Cal has made many return trips to the temple with his faithful companion, Dumbo. Once there, he is given a book which, when opened, fills his awareness with vivid images, some obscure and some teaching pointed lessons.

He has grown in faith, hope, and love. He has broken through the barrier of his father's ignorance of love which he had made his own. Having found hidden treasure in himself, he now looks for and values it in others.

He wants to live because he wants to practice giving and receiving love. He wants to become good at it. He sees depression as a hindrance and takes anti-depressant medication.

The lump in his neck, whatever it was, disappeared after his first trip to the Temple.

The Veiled Lady

Marlene's Daimon appeared to her unbidden while she was working with imagery to reduce her depression. As has happened in numerous cases, the Daimon entered the scene as Healer and went on to teach the client transcendence.

Although she was not conscious of the dynamics, there was little mystery to me about why this woman in her late thirties was becoming increasingly depressed. She believed it was her bounden duty to meet all the needs of her husband and children while being at the same time committed to perfect performance in her role as a legal secretary. It never occurred to her to say no to any request from important people in her life.

A technique frequently helpful to people like her is called "symptom imagery." The client is taught relaxation and instructed to invite his or her Unconscious to project an image that represents the presenting symptom, in this instance, depression.

The image that flashed immediately into Marlene's awareness was a set of barbells. They were shiny black and huge. Though she thought the image to be ridiculous, I encouraged her to work with it as a metaphor for her depression.

At my request she imagined herself in proximity to the barbells. Then I asked what she felt like doing with them or about them. At this point, many choices were available to her. Revealingly, she decided to pick them up.

Though she described the weights as oversize, she began to struggle with them. The muscle tension in her arms and some grunting confirmed that the imagery had become her reality of the moment.

When she declared she was getting nowhere, I asked her to take a break and consider what she wanted to do. Wouldn't you know, she decided to go back to the lifting.

This time, as she exerted even more effort, she became aware of being watched by a soft, pretty woman dressed in a plain, long gown with a mantilla draped over her head and trailing across her shoulders. Very firmly the woman said, "Stop!"

Marlene was awestruck by this unexpected turn in the imaginary events. The woman drew closer holding out a handkerchief. She told her to wipe the sweat from her face and relax.

I was as surprised as my client but sensed that the figure was of great importance. I instructed Marlene to ask the woman's name. It was Veronica. She said she had come with an important message. The message was: It's all right to just let go.

Veronica went on to say that, while everyone must fulfill responsibilities and bear burdens in life, Marlene was neglecting her "precious inner being" (soul?) in doing for others. She instructed her to "lighten her load."

"Follow me," she said, "and I will show you the gentle face of God."

The abruptness with which all of this came forth told me that Marlene had tapped into her higher consciousness. The wisdom spoken by Veronica immediately "sank in." Following this integration of the image's message, Marlene was able to better control her co-dependency and to reserve some of her time and energy for herself. With Veronica as her guide, she began her spiritual journey.

Shortly after her first meeting with her Daimon, I asked Marlene if she knew anything about St. Veronica. Born and raised Baptist, she was not well indoctrinated regarding the pantheon of saints. She claimed no conscious awareness of one called Veronica.

I encouraged her to research the First Century St. Veronica and she was dumbfounded to discover that she was known for greeting Jesus as he paused while bearing his cross to Mt. Calvary. Legend has it she offered him her veil to wipe his bloody, sweaty face and that an image of his face was left on the cloth.

The parallels between her image and the legend were striking. Her Veronica also wore a veil and offered a face wiping cloth as Marlene set aside her "heavy burden." Her Veronica promised to show her the "gentle face of God."

During one of her imagery sessions Marlene asked Veronica if she were the same person who appeared in the Bible story. She received an answer in the affirmative.

I do not know who or what these imaged entities are. I know only that they have their own energy, a body of wisdom that exceeds what Ego knows, and that they speak the language of the Divine.

The stories of Cal and Marlene, like many others in this volume, demonstrate that many times mental and emotional illnesses are linked to a spiritual crisis that is not directly perceived by the patient. In Spiritual Emergency (1989), Stan and Christina Grof expound on the idea that many mental aberrations are events reflecting the evolvement of an individual's consciousness to a higher spiritual level. Unfortunately, there are many therapists who are just as blind to this as their patients.

CHAPTER THIRTEEN

The Mythic Gift

I celebrate myself, and sing myself.

- Walt Whitman
- Song of Myself

Some of the time, Daimon is in an adversarial role with Ego. As champion of the Soul and representative of the non-material universe he is bound to find himself in conflict with Ego's sometimes arrogant insistence on being in control and knowing all there is to know.

In the end, however, the Daimon presents a gift that is just as vital to the Ego as the Soul. This gift is a story authored by the Daimon which tells us and others who we are in our essence.

The story is unique because of the very special way the Daimon chronicles our lives. He presents us to ourselves and others in the role of the mythic hero. In short, he creates for us our personal myth, an account of who and what we are that transcends the mundane circumstances of our day to day existence.

Myths And Lies

In popular usage the word "myth" connotes a tale or a legend that is patently false. More accurately, myths are stories that point to truths that lie beyond their content. They serve to reveal the deeper meaning and purpose of life.

Thus, the body of literature known as mythology encompasses the world's great sacred texts and treatises on humankind's relationship to the Divine. Our own Bible belongs in this category.

The notion of myths as falsehoods undoubtedly grows out of our tendency to look upon other people's religion as unfounded or misguided while seeing our own as divinely inspired and unquestionably valid. This is unfortunate for, while myths are non-factual or only partly factual, they are true.

A myth is a unique kind of story that imparts to an individual or an entire societal system eternal truths and the meaning of existence. Myths generated and perpetuated by a particular culture are usually based on the exploits of God or the gods or some extraordinary mortal. In regard to the latter, the events of an historical person's life are usually exaggerated and enhanced by legendary material, imparting to the individual god-like attributes. Religious figures like Confucius, Moses, Jesus, Mohammed, Buddha, and the Virgin Mary are examples of humans who have been mythologized.

Though they may be characterized as super-human rather than as gods, this same phenomenon takes place in regard to people from the fields of entertainment, politics, sports, and other endeavors which bestow star status on someone. George Washington, Knute Rockne, Florence Nightingale, Abraham Lincoln, George Custer, Elvis Presley, Jesse James, John Chapman (Johnny Appleseed), Davy Crockett, Amelia Earhart, and Marilyn Monroe are just a few examples of American celebrities whose lives have been mythologized.

The great myths that have been passed down through the ages with multi-generational impact have served to answer the big questions that have confronted us since the dawn of consciousness. They tell us who we are. They establish our identity by showing us our place in the panoramic scheme of life and by explicating our relationship to the forces that control life.

These great myths also serve to make us aware of the origin and importance of "our people" whomever they may be. Myths of this nature focus on topics such as "us Smiths," "us Californians," "us Catholics," "us Marines," "us Americans," etc. They bind us more closely to those who share our bloodlines, viewpoints, and experiences.

These are the myths that teach us values that, when shared with others, become part of our group bond. From that group's perspective, they define good behavior and cite its rewards. They also set forth the consequences of failing to adhere to the moral code.

Of primary importance are the cultural myths that provide us with a representation of the ongoing process of creation. Usually beginning with an account of the origin of the universe, they proceed to embody the mysteries of creation in its varied forms.

As repositories of these truths, regardless of their factual content, the myths of each particular culture are treasured by that culture. The cultural fiber is weakened without them.

Our Judeo/Christian Bible has been one of the few mythic writings to get widespread attention in modern North American culture. Today, it is rejected or ignored by great numbers of people, leaving us in the unenviable position of becoming an essentially mythless society.

The Good Book As Good Myth

As a sacred text the Bible fulfills all the requirements of mythological writings and is full of rich imagery, mystery, and wisdom. Factually it is full of errors and distortions. Parts of it are blatant fabrications. In terms of its mythological function, this does not matter.

Its decline of influence in our society has come about in large part because it is not accepted as myth by many members of the Christian Churches. Moreover, mythology itself is not accepted as an enriching, enlightening body of wisdom suitable for guiding, counseling, and directing our lives and the lives of others outside of the Church.

You are bound to be well aware of the many proponents of the Word who will not countenance putting the Bible in the same category with the other great sacred texts of the world. There are those who hold that recognition or acknowledgment of its falsehoods, inaccuracies, and editorial enhancements would destroy its value. They proceed either to overlook or deny its errors or to render them correct through rationalizations and spurious interpretations.

Those who are zealous about proving the factual validity of the scriptures are not apt to promote the adventure and enlightenment to be found in exploring them as a treasury of wisdom. In some minds, especially those of Church indoctrinated Christians, it is profane to read the gospel accounts of Jesus' life as anything other than an accurate biography dictated by God him/herself.

In spite of the importance some people attach to the historical veracity of the gospels, one can read with no illusions the most dubious sections like Luke's Christmas legend and be deeply moved by its beauty and its message of God's love coming into the world. The truths expressed are much grander and more compelling than the historical details of the narrative. This is the essence of myth.

Ultimately, insistence on treating the Bible as a book of facts has diminished its impact on our culture but it is not the only factor. Another is the rise in the Twentieth Century of scientism with its rejection of the value of myth. The bottom line is that we have no widely shared cultural myth and, without it, our collective sense of identity has become vague.

The Star of Bethlehem has long since faded from the sky. The heroes of our wars are buried and forgotten. The astronauts have become mere mortals. We have been reduced to a generation of seekers groping about in the faint glow of pocket flashlights. Occasionally we catch in our beam heroic figures like the gallant police officers and firefighters of the World Trade Center, but eventually the light grows dim.

No wonder we have at the end of the millenium factions seeking to post the Ten Commandments on classroom walls and to make school prayer mandatory. Though I find these particular practices objectionable, I view them as attempts to bring a shared mythology back into our culture. They are misguided in the sense that this cannot be accomplished through legislation or force.

When we all swore by the same Book we were narcissistically enabled to envision ourselves and others like us as cohorts of the gods. With no widely shared heroes or body of ethics our attitude toward ourselves becomes demeaning. We become inconsequential in our own eyes.

We need to locate ourselves somewhere between two extremes. My awareness is that we are unique creatures who live at the interface between the dirt and the heavens, a position which permits us to play a vital role in the evolution of God and his/her universe.

It is not that we are totally without larger than life mythic figures to emulate but they have lost their sacred quality. Today we tend to find them in our literature, music, on television, and at the movies.

They are temporarily exciting but like meteors soon fade on the horizon. They are so many in number and so time limited that they capture the attention of segments of society while contributing little or nothing to the cohesiveness of the whole social structure. If they strengthen our sense of connectedness at all, it is to a few others only.

Without a widely shared mythology our bond to others is weakened. Our sense of a shared moral code diminishes. Our appreciation of all things created is weakened. The environment is devalued and our willingness to exploit it grows more ruthless.

We need myths to live. We need myths to live by.

The Vital Myth

In order to survive the demise of our cultural myth, one essential myth must sustain us. This is our personal myth.

Creating a personal myth is one of the basic functions of the Daimon. Personal myth is not the same as the chronological history of our existence which all of us carry around in our head. The latter is a record of the main events of our lives based on our recall of the facts surrounding them.

The Daimon's personal myth incorporates the ingredients of all myths. It is a reconstruction of our life in the form of a drama that is full of meanings more grand and sweeping than the day to day events might suggest.

It is based, in common with our chronological history, on our life experiences but it emphasizes the meaning and significance of those experiences much more than the details describing the exact circumstances surrounding them. It ties our experience to our dreams, imaginings, and inner explorations. It reveals simultaneously the heroic aspects of our pilgrimage through the external and internal realms realities of our existence.

The Daimon stores in memory our lived adventures and writes them large in our mythic journal. He records therein the extraordinary features (and there always are some) of our birth and childhood.

He notes our battles with sickness and hardship. He describes the family that raised us with its loves, conflicts, jealousies, abuses, tenderness, and joys. He recounts the drama of our transformation from child to adult during the tumultuous years of adolescence.

He chronicles our feats and foibles, successes and failures, highs and lows, gains and losses. He traces our encounters with the mysteries of sex, our mastery of occupational and social skills, our way of expressing citizenship in our community and the world at large.

He reflects upon our experience with romantic love, commitment, aggression, kindness, pain, aging, and death. He acknowledges the other personal myths that have helped to shape our own. In the end, our myth reveals us to be imperfect yet magnificent beings - the stuff heroes are made of.

The Mythologization Of Melinda

Some Daimons are so thoroughly squelched during childhood that they are unable to or are substantially delayed in bringing to an individual an awareness of his or her mythic attributes. My client, Melinda, was just such a person.

In Melinda's family of origin, her authoritarian father reigned supreme. Her mother assumed a role of complete subservience to her husband and Melinda's two younger brothers. In this household the only creatures of value and importance were males.

Females were treated like and expected to act like second class citizens. By family definition, females were powerless, devoid of magical qualities.

Being the oldest and only female child, Melinda was expected to slave side by side with her mother on behalf of the men in the family. Responsibilities for maintenance of the home, including domestic services and taking charge of her brothers, fell on her shoulders from an early age. She learned while still a toddler that the first priority in life was to please father.

This was not easily done because Melinda's father was as critical as he was controlling. He gave no praise and never failed to verbalize unkind epithets about his wife and daughter when things didn't go to his liking.

Father ordained that the boys should be well educated, prosperous businessmen like himself. He carefully planned and financed their schooling. He showed no interest in Melinda's desire for a career in Library Science, insisting it would be a waste of money to send her to a good university because she would "just get married in a year or two."

The girl ended up attending the community college in her hometown and, as father had predicted, was married after completing the two-year program. The man she married was the easy-going antithesis of her father. Melinda reveled in his non-critical attitude, failing to note that he was also devoid of ambition and quite irresponsible.

Within the first five years of marriage she had given birth to two children and was faced with the necessity of having to get a job. All the while, she continued to faithfully visit her parents and, when in their home, waited on her father just as attentively as she had in the past.

In keeping with her basic training, she fulfilled all of these responsibilities without joy and without complaint. All of her hurt, anger, and sadness was kept inside under a tight lid.

When Melinda was thirty-six her father suffered a back injury which led to spinal surgery and a long convalescence. Her mother was stressed to the breaking point by trying to care for her even more than usually demanding and ungrateful husband. Like the dutiful daughter she had always been, Melinda took on the added responsibility of helping her mother with household chores and taking a hot meal to her parents' home three nights a week so her mother could get more rest.

The father, continuing his pattern of behavior full force, made a special point of criticizing the food his daughter brought to them. He "kidded" his wife for having failed to teach Melinda how to cook, saying he guessed he was going to have to give her lessons himself. He called several of the dishes she brought to them "slop" even as he ate them. He said he was surprised Melinda's husband remained in the marriage if this was the kind of stuff she gave him to eat.

One evening, when he was in more pain than usual and his mood was particularly foul, the old man railed to such an extent that Melinda broke into tears, whereupon he chided her for "acting just like a woman" and told her to "knock it off." When she could not control her crying he became more abusive and, calling her emotional display "sickening," he proceeded to dump his full plate of food into his bedside trash can.

It was the crowning event of years of torment. Long repressed Daimonic energy was released with a force of mythic proportions. Melinda, for the first time in her life, was about to become the Hero.

Later, in therapy, she told me she literally felt something inside of her snap when her father dumped his plate. A guttural scream spontaneously escaped from her throat.

She marched to the bedside and yelled, "You son-of-a-bitch!" With that, she picked up the bedside trashcan and heaped its contents right into her father's bedridden lap.

For a moment, the never before challenged master of the house was apoplectic. When he finally caught his breath, he called wildly to his wife, saying Melinda had gone crazy and instructing her to summon the police immediately. The woman was too dumbfounded to respond.

Melinda, feeling strong and self assured, turned and walked out of the house. All the way to her car she could hear her father hysterically screaming "Maniac! Maniac!" repeatedly.

That moment of high drama marked the emergence of Melinda's mythic self. She had slain the Dragon; she had survived the Ordeal of Fire. From that point on and forevermore she and those with whom she was intimate would know her as the woman who triumphed over her father, a reputation not unlike that of Jack the Giant Killer.

After the dumping episode, Melinda's life story was no longer just a footnote to that of her parents. She was separate - known for her courage - important in her own right. The usual guilt and fear about displeasing her father did not overtake her this time though her father has ever since refused to speak to her. Nor did she weaken when her mother begged her to apologize to the old tyrant lest she be dropped from his will.

The myth that is Melinda has continued to grow. She insisted that her husband get a second job so she could go back to college. She has done well academically.

Like all Heroes our mythic self undergoes many transformations. Metaphorically, the mythic self encounters many dragons and, in doing battle with them, may be repeatedly torn apart. Each time, he nonetheless re-members who he is and returns stronger and more skilled in dragon fighting. Each new slaying of the beast transports the Hero to a higher level of development.

Living Someone Else's Myth

Problems arise when we attempt to live out the myth another has written for us. This occurs in family units wherein individual members assign a mythic role to one or more persons within their ranks.

When a young woman named Lila consulted me for therapy just prior to the Christmas season, she was troubled by the sudden onset of anxiety attacks. She was not aware that she was in the throes of a mythic transformation.

A few months before our initial contact, Lila's younger sister had been killed in an accident while boating with her boyfriend. Though deeply affected by her sister's death, Lila had openly displayed very little grief. She had maintained a facade of calm and strength so the other family members could lean on her.

In the course of our discussion it was brought to light that Lila, the oldest child, had long ago been designated by her parents and herself to be "the strong one in the family." By embracing this persona she had derived gratifying feelings of being worthwhile and needed. She was living the mythic role of Wonder Woman so that others in the family could be mere mortals.

She was so praised for this performance that she learned from an early age to repress her quite human and intense emotional responses to life's adversities. She came to believe she was, indeed, an "iron willed, indestructible" individual. Her soft side became her Shadow.

177

She looked contemptuously upon "snivelers" even as she nurtured them.

It didn't take long for Lila to figure out that her current anxiety had been precipitated by a growing fear that she might experience a breakthrough of emotions during the traditional family Christmas gathering where her sister's absence would be felt by all. She could not bear the thought of appearing to be "weak' in the presence of her parents, siblings, and other relatives. She and they, she thought, needed her to be controlled and in charge as always.

As Lila became more aware of the myth she was living, the door opened for her to get in touch with feelings she had heretofore been avoiding. She discovered that a part of herself was more Margaret O'Brien than John Wayne. Helping her to reconcile these opposites was the main thrust of our therapeutic work.

Lila believed that giving in to her own need for comfort and support would totally negate her established identity within the family. Inwardly she both desired and feared revealing her "neediness." She envisioned becoming a blubbering mass of uncontrolled emotion who, thenceforth, would never be regarded as a strong, capable person.

Happily, the therapeutic experience helped this client discover that getting in touch with her Shadow side and allowing it expression made her feel more rather than less powerful. She found her anxiety diminishing as she began to fully verbalize her fears and sorrows.

Before presents were exchanged on Christmas Eve, Lila proposed a loving toast to her absent sister and bawled like a baby. She cried longer and harder than some of the others.

To her surprise, her relatives responded to her with heartfelt displays of affection and respect. As they comforted her, several said that her revelation of her emotions had given them permission to release their own. Her favorite brother told her that he thought she had demonstrated "great strength" by breaking down.

Moments of Passage And Heroes

The personal myth is founded on what might be called moments of passage in our lives. Melinda's transformation from victim to dragon slayer and Lila's heroic revelation of her not so mighty, grieving Child are good examples of what I mean.

Both women crossed lines that redefined for themselves and others who they were. Melinda thereafter was looked upon by herself and others as an effectively assertive person. Lila's identity expanded to include her vulnerable, emotional Child. Undoubtedly, other moments of passage preceded the ones recounted here and many more came after.

The mythological viewpoint is similar to that of the alchemists of yore who sought, through a series of chemical refinements, to transform ordinary matter into gold. The personal myth dramatizes our being processed into finer stuff through a series of transforming life experiences.

Our movement through the various bio-psycho-socio-spiritual stages of life affords ample opportunity for heroic adaptations and change even if the events are quite commonplace. At each of these junctures we must make choices, take risks, and experience loss or gain. The heroic aspect is not defined by the nobility of our acts or a favorable outcome. It is defined by the mettle we show as we encounter the dragon of the moment. These passages move us from one state of being to another or one level of awareness to a higher one and usually pivot around a single, dramatic event.

I have a personal rite of passage story that I think well illustrates the mythic component. It somewhat glorifies aggression but I assure you that other lessons at other times forcefully taught me the drawbacks of aggressive behavior. It probably fairly represents a typical kind of trial that most male children in our society face in some form at some point in their developmental life.

By way of background it is important that you know I was a sickly child (in adulthood I came to realize my never well defined ailments were mostly psychophysiological) with no strong male influence in my preadolescent years. I had no concept of possessing physical strength and no experience of being confrontational with my peers.

Given this mind-set, it is no wonder that I managed to project a "Kick Me" message to the world and was frequently the target of bullies. Believing myself to be far too weak and helpless to fight back, I compensated by developing some skill at running away. My passive and aggressive traits were so out of balance that I and others could only identify me as a victim supreme.

During my early years, I played happily alone much of the time. My closest friend was a gentle little neighbor girl named Mary Jo. I loved her dearly and still remember her with affection. We took care of our family of stuffed animals, captured insects (some of which I would not touch with a long stick today), and acted out things we saw in the movies.

As wonderful as our relationship was, it afforded me no opportunity to invest in so-called "boy things." Rough and tumble sports and play were totally unknown to me.

When I was ten, my parents and I moved to Atlanta and changes ensued. My heretofore absentee father and I began doing some things together. I learned a little about football and baseball and, to my surprise, discovered I had some modest athletic skills. Gradually, I began to evolve a more typically "masculine" orientation.

In Atlanta, the children of the neighborhood were boys of my age. My contacts with them were tentative at first but, with one, I soon struck what was to be an enduring friendship. With the other, I established a mutually jealous rivalry.

Pat, my rival, liked to provoke me. He recognized that I was not especially adventuresome and reveled in calling me "chicken" at every opportunity. I found that label to be particularly odious but, of course, locked my lips and put up with it.

The big-time activity in those days was playing marbles. In the yard outside of our apartment building, we drew our rings in the areas devoid of grass and took our shots at each other's prize specimens.

We argued heavily on almost every play. After all, we were playing for keeps and some favorite agates were usually part of the stakes.

On a fall day during one of our many harangues over some technicality, Pat got hysterical. Saying, "I quit," in a rage he grabbed up several of my prize marbles along with his own and refused to return them to me on request. God knows what forces were operative at that moment but, for the first time in my life, I decided I wasn't going to let myself be jerked around.

Through clenched teeth I said, "Give me back my marbles, Pat!" My voice was just a little shrill. Images of John Wayne handling an unruly out-of-line cowpoke were flashing on my inner movie screen.

Pat shook his skinny fist at me. "No! And you can't do anything about it!" was his defiant comeback.

A sense of being on the verge of something momentous washed over me. The drama was heightened when I caught a glimpse of the gorgeous high school junior who lived in one of the downstairs apartments peering out at us through her living room window. At that tender age I regarded her as a sex goddess and there she was, following our confrontation with apparent interest.

The verbal exchanges continued and became more threatening. I prolonged the arguing as a means of stalling while I desperately tried to figure out what to do next. Pat was just my size but the idea of attacking anyone larger than Tweety Bird was completely alien to me. It was beginning to appear I would either have to use force or slink away in cowardly defeat. Recollections of past humiliations at the hands of bullies flooded my consciousness.

"O.K., Pat, this is your last chance." My voice now resonated with great resolve. "Hand over my marbles or I'm going to take them."

The boy's cherry red face twisted up in a tight little scowl. Contemptuously he shouted, "You won't do anything about it. You're chicken!"

That did it. He had used the C word. Too much was at stake: the reputation for being chicken, the marbles, the admiration of the fair damsel at the window. Years of pent-up aggression blew the floodgates. Shazam! The perennial victim became Captain Marvel.

I ran full speed at my antagonist until I felt my shoulder connect with his mid-section. The wind whooshed out of him and he went over, spilling his marbles.

I put a headlock on him until he cried, "I give up!"

In ecstasy over my newfound strength I made him say it three times loudly.

When I relinquished my hold, Pat continued to lie with his face in the dirt, crying. I told him not to move while I picked up my purloined marbles and he obeyed.

Putting my darlings back in the sock in which I carried them, I paused for a moment, standing over my vanquished nemesis. Then I strode triumphantly away, dazzled by my own display of power.

With a cautious sideways glance, I checked to see if the girl was still at her window. Not only was she still watching but when she caught my gaze she raised her hands in mock applause. I could feel my cheeks grow hot as I swaggered back to my apartment.

Primitive maybe but it was definitely a mythic moment. It was just what I needed at that particular point in time, just as I needed instruction in humility at other times. It was a moment in which I discovered a side of myself I had never known.

I had stood up for my rights. I had acted aggressively toward another human being. I had won the day and the favor of the beautiful lady. Never again would I define myself as weak and helpless. I was, at last, the hero of my own myth.

CHAPTER FOURTEEN

Joy, Pain, and Spirited Imagination

A Spirit gripped him by the hair and carried him far away,
Till he heard as the roar of a rain-fed ford the roar of the
Milky Way.

> \- Rudyard Kipling
> Tomlinson

Those of us who allow the Daimon to lead us in pursuit of the Gleam may find ourselves like Kipling's (1989) Tomlinson carried to ethereal heights. However, we should keep in mind that the title character of this poem was taken in another direction as well:

"The Spirit gripped him by the hair, and sun by sun they fell
Till they came to the belt of Naughty Stars that rim the mouth of Hell."

The Daimon's vision encompasses both the sacred and profane. We cannot have it one way only. The ecstasy of awakening to wonders and communing with the Divine is laced with fear and trembling.

All of the miracles we have cited have their dark side. The winds and rains that cool and refresh us can reach hurricane force and cut a swath of destruction. The gentle animal that licks our hand still carries within the instinctive potential for attack. The miracle of birth may bring us face to face with a monstrous mistake of Nature.

We can be healed and later suffer a more dreadful malady. We can forgive and receive contempt for our forgiveness. We can love and be rejected. And the final wonder of all, death, can bring with it torment and terror before it delivers us.

Spirit directed imagination brings enchantment into our life, not safety. It fills us with awe, not ease.

183

We are spared nothing of life's harshness by following the Gleam. The Daimon's path is just as much one of hot sands and jagged stones as meadows and quiet streams. The difficult passages are rendered even more agonizing because our travels constantly teach us to be more sensitive to our own pain and that of others.

So, why do we bother to make the trip?

Most of us invest a great deal of planning, energy, and money in vacations. Ego wants to view the wonders of the physical world and re-create in places of beauty, havens of love, arenas of excitement, or playgrounds for the Child. Generally, there is great joy in these endeavors but it is not unusual to observe Ego, soon after the visit is complete, planning the next great adventure, sure to be even more fulfilling.

Soul thirsts for the spiritual counterparts of all this. She wants to view spiritual wonders and re-create in the inner landscapes, to seek beauty and love in pure form, to be challenged and offered risks, and to return the Child at last to its paradisal origin. In these pursuits lies the joy of the Soul. At each new plateau she begins to anticipate new discoveries and journeys farther afield. The Gleam lies always just over the horizon.

For both Ego and Soul it is the striving, the almost attaining, which makes the journey worthwhile. The fleeting moments of fulfillment entice both to make their pilgrimages again and again.

Everybody knows pain. Buddha identified suffering as the basic element of life. It is intrinsic to existence. It goes with the territory. Ego seeks means of avoiding it; Soul seeks to transcend it. Both must endure it.

How we relate to pain is a measure of our character, our courage, and our faith.

Victims: Real And Wannabes

Throughout our travels with the Daimon our bodies suffer the inevitable ravages of time while our psyches are becoming more integrated. Pain contributes to our psychospiritual growth. If we are to regard the experience of pain as essential to completeness, we are called to be cautious in estimating the degree of victimization occurring in our own life and the lives of others.

This is my basis for declaring that diseases, disasters, losses, aging, and death itself are wonders, even as they are sources of suffering. They are wonders because we could not connect fully with the experience of being human without them. It may be that we could not imagine God without them.

Without pain, how motivated would we be to evolve as individuals? In recognizing the growth opportunity imbedded in pain we are compelled to examine one of the most prevalent and insidious disorders of our time: victim mentality.

The Daimon, in the course of her travel between the material and spiritual realms of reality, is in an excellent position to address the three most pertinent questions relating to victimization:

1. How much of the bad that happens in our lives is the work of forces completely beyond our control?
2. How much is caused by the actions and attitudes of others?
3. How much is the result of our own doing?

Each individual will respond to these questions differently. Subjective beliefs and perceptions will have a strong bearing on their answers. Some of us validly and some invalidly feel more victimized than others.

My own image of a pure victim is someone upon whom a meteor falls. This assumes that the person was making every reasonable effort to avoid the thing. Any of us can become victims of a natural disaster but folks who go out of doors for a stroll during a storm or take a swim when lightning is about are hardly bona fide victims.

Certain classes of beings are more vulnerable to victimization than others. Animals, children, the aged, and the physically and mentally handicapped are prime examples. Women are at unacceptably high risk to become victims of physical abuse and rape at the hands of men.

In addition, there are authentic victims of social/political injustice such as the Jews of the Holocaust and those ethnic and religious groups that are the targets of despots or hate mongers. At one time or another, most of us have been perpetrators, recipients, or observers of victimization through prejudice, sexual bias, unfair employment practices, or personal favoritism. We have probably also encountered people who claimed to be victimized when they were not.

There are also victims of other people's irresponsibility or insanity. Conceivably, any of us could fall before the maniac who opens fire with an automatic weapon in a crowded mall, the unseen bomber who sets off an explosion in a terminal, the hijacker who commandeers an aircraft, or the drunk driver who swerves into our lane of traffic. September 11, 2001, brought home to Americans inclined toward complacency that none of us are immune to terrorism.

On the other hand, can we legitimately claim victimization if we insist on visiting a country that our State Department declares unsafe? What if we pick up a hitchhiker who turns out to be a serial killer or get punched in the face while frequenting a place where people consume too much alcohol?

There is what I consider to be an unfortunate societal trend toward not holding people responsible for their choices and actions. Perpetrators of crime are frequently defended in court and exonerated on the grounds of their own victimization.

Capital offenders are portrayed as victims of a sordid childhood. Murderers are proclaimed to be victims of momentary insanity. Smokers (notwithstanding the despicable tactics of the tobacco industry) claim to be victims of advertising, and delinquents are represented as victims of television programming.

In today's world there is a sizeable population of victim wannabes. Achieving victim status has resulted in handsome financial rewards for many. Others use it to avoid blame for their actions or to justify poor choices or an irresponsible lifestyle.

In his thought-provoking book, <u>Evil: Inside Human Violence and Cruelty</u>, Roy Baumeister (1999) concludes that evil acts of aggression are spawned within the depths of human nature. Culture can mitigate or exacerbate this tendency but the baseline deterrent is the internal restraints that the individual has built in.

Choice And Risk

Unhappily, I must admit that the field of psychotherapy has contributed to our society's "poor old Jack the Ripper" mentality. In our effort to develop a compassionate understanding of human behavior we therapists have somehow managed to convince some people that they should not be held accountable for the consequences of their choices.

There is very little we do that does not involve choice making at some level. We owe it to ourselves to make informed choices and to be prepared to live with the consequences, whether they turn out for better or worse.

The Daimon, the part of us that chooses to believe the unbelievable, is aware of the ongoing process of choice- making in our lives. The Daimon influences that process with intuitive guidance. The Ego participates in the process with rational input. Other personality components would have us make choices based on responses programmed into us during our developmental years. We need to be conscious of all these sources in our decision making.

No matter how carefully we weigh our choices, the fact remains that there are no guaranteed outcomes. The price of taking extraordinary precautions to avoid risk may be an existence that is numbingly boring. The price of throwing caution to the winds may be a brief but exciting visit to Planet Earth. Either way, it is our destiny to end up dead.

Responsible living calls upon us to maintain clarity regarding the part we play in bringing that destiny to fruition. This includes maintaining an awareness of how we help to create the bad things that happen in our lives.

Aside from enabling certain people to avoid responsibility for their behavior by placing causal blame on some outside influence, the field of psychotherapy has poorly served many legitimate victims. There are therapists who so centralize their client's experience of victimization as to convince him/her that it is the source of everything that is wrong - past, present and future. They take the position that the damage wrought by victimization is so great that recovery should not be expected. In this scenario, the client's primary identity becomes "victim."

Surviving extraordinary hardships should and does become a mythic quality to which an individual should lay claim as noted in the previous chapter. However, it is emotionally crippling to identify this as the last or, perhaps, only great life-act of which an individual can boast. This is particularly pathetic if the concept of "survivor" carries with it a label of "permanent damage." The should be proud survivor is relegated to the demoralizing company of similarly damaged souls whose lives are dedicated to "living with a handicap that makes coping with life difficult or impossible."

Victim mentality fosters a perception of life being a situation in which:

"Things happen to me. I am powerless. Others push me around. God zaps me. I can only wait and see what happens to me next. If only (life event X) had never happened. Nobody ever gets over something like that."

God save us from the therapists.

The Delights And Miseries Of Pain

Nothing is more apt to trigger in us a sense of victimization than pain. One of the triumphs of medical science is its ability to keep us relatively free of pain through the administration of drugs. Even as we are thankful for this, we need to recognize that it as a mixed blessing. Many in our society lose tolerance for any degree of discomfort and become overly dependent on the medicines that relieve it.

We can benefit from an awareness of the creative element in pain. It is, after all, our nervous system's way of telling us there is something wrong with us and/or our life-space. If we don't rush unreflectively to get it stopped via drugs or surgery we can learn something from it.

Pain is a messenger.

This brings to mind a woman who did learn from her pain after years of resentfully waiting for some doctor to alleviate it. Her name was Phyllis and she became my client after consulting one physician then another about her varied aches and pains, most of which were of vague origin. She had headaches, muscular aches, joint aches, and stomachaches in addition to experiencing prolonged and inordinate pain over the slightest injury.

When I first met Phyllis I could hardly get her to talk of anything but her pain. Her discourses on the subject made it obvious that she thought some metaphysical entity was giving her a very raw deal and that her doctors were further victimizing her by not giving a damn about her plight. She was full of anger because no one seemed to want to pay attention to her suffering.

It was easy to establish the validity of that last allegation. In our very first session, I too felt an immediate desire to escape from her barrage of pain talk.

After listening to her tale of woe for a few minutes, even the most sympathetic person would try to change the subject but Phyllis had a talent for returning again and again to the topic of her pain. I had occasion to observe her in some social situations and noted that, upon meeting someone, she would manage within three to five minutes to let the person know she was suffering exquisite pain.

She might as well have made it her way of introducing herself. "Hello, I'm Phyllis. I'm in terrible pain." You can imagine how attractive this was to others.

It took a long while and a lot of patience to get Phyllis interested in looking at pain as a mystery shrouded message which was making a bid to enter her consciousness. She finally called forth her Daimon as Inner Guide when it dawned on her that her dependency on medication had become a threat to her health and that she had better try a new approach.

The first thing her Guide, a German Shepherd named Watchdog (Phyllis was not fond of dogs), revealed to her was that her pain was more psychological than physical. He led her to a high peak from which she could look down on her daily life. She saw herself feeling responsible for the problems of others. She took care of sick people, chauffeured little old ladies around town, served on church committees, and was never known to say "no" when asked to do something. This was the mythic person she had been scripted to be by her parents.

It came as a revelation to Phyllis when she discovered that she really hated about ninety percent of all her good deed doing. From the time of her childhood she had never felt that anyone paid enough attention to her or made an effort to take care of her. It seemed to her that, in all of her relationships throughout life, she had ended up being the attention giver and caretaker. During her working years she had been - guess what - a nurse.

For a long time, she kept her resentment repressed but she consciously felt heavily burdened by her many responsibilities. She got no sense of wonder out of what she was contributing but did not feel worthwhile enough to demand time and attention for herself.

Unable to admit to herself or to others that she didn't like her responsibilities, Phyllis unconsciously developed a reliance on pain to get her out of things and to justify focusing on herself.

While continuing to outwardly appear eagerly all giving, she let everyone know she had limits by telling them repeatedly of her pain problem. Knowing of it, who could blame this martyred, self-sacrificing, pain ridden woman if she occasionally failed to follow through on some commitments? Who would not marvel at her selflessness?

This woman's pain was not an invention but it was psychologically advantageous for her to maximize and capitalize on her somatogenic pain. It was her way of justifying certain "selfish" behaviors that would otherwise make her a bad person in her own eyes. This worked satisfactorily as long as she didn't realize what she was doing. Once she developed insight into the matter it became difficult for her to maintain her stance as a total victim of pain.

With her Daimon revitalized, Phyllis began to think and act creatively. She began pursuing her suppressed interest in computers and got herself a PC. She soon discovered she was a computer whiz and began to spend more time in serious interaction with her McIntosh. Lo and behold, during her hours in front of the screen, she was completely unmindful of pain.

Along with her appreciation of the wonders of cyberspace, she acquired the ability to say "no." She demanded more time for herself and found some ways to make a little money with her skills. She did not achieve total freedom from pain but she began to feel in control of it and was able to get along without any prescription drugs for it.

Though she suffered much, in the end Phyllis gained much from confronting her pain instead of running away from it. She finally got its message.

The Wonder Of Loss

Catastrophic events, sickness, and pain are not the only sources of victimized feelings. Our losses generate them just as readily.

In <u>Necessary Losses</u>, Judith Viorst (1986) contends that the inevitable series of losses that permeate all our lives are the vehicles by which we evolve toward greater maturity and wisdom. For all the grief they bring to us, they have a positive value.

It is in coping with loss that our personhood is established. Losses provide us with essential opportunities to forge our character structure along both positive and negative lines.

This is not the popular viewpoint. Citizens of the Twenty-first Century take pride and satisfaction in believing that we have a tremendous amount of control over what happens in our lives. They trust technology and the omniscient experts to fix everything.

Take note of how many people are totally aghast when natural disasters and inadvertent tragedies strike. They immediately start to ask their questions:

How could this happen? Why? Why to me? You mean there is no remedy? No prevention? No treatment? Whose fault is this?

Belief that everything is potentially fixable leads us to be intensely resentful about our losses. Somebody out there should have seen it coming and done something. We feel we have been slighted. Our revered experts have dropped the ball.

Especially when it occurs close to home, many of us are determined that it should nearly always be possible to alleviate suffering, even to prevent death. We confidently administer drugs and hook up elaborate apparatuses to those who falter but still there is suffering and still there is death. In spite of all we know, this is how it is and how it will remain for ages to come.

Lots of people are in denial. They don't want to hear this. They believe that a lifetime of losses is meaningless or, worse, a form of torture. They question the use of trying in a world where all you do is suffer and die.

These are the ones who made popular the bumper sticker of the 80's that read, "Life's a bitch and then you die." They don't want to look for meaning in suffering and dying. If suffering and dying can't be eradicated, life is a rip-off.

The Daimon approaches impermanence and loss with gentle acquiescence. His message is that we are all pilgrims with no possessions who borrow the things of the world during our brief journey through it. Everyone and everything dear to us is made that much more precious by virtue of being on loan to us for the passing of life's short day. Within this framework, the Daimon deeply appreciates the beauty of all things created which are all things perishable. He recognizes his kinship with all.

Many of the great mystics of both East and West have retired to the wilderness to live among the animals in order to advance their spiritual growth. Meister Eckhart preached that all creatures are a divine blessing and a direct revelation of the Creator. There were those like Francis of Assisi, the saint known for calling all things in nature his brothers and sisters, and exalting creation even when he was living in absolutely wretched physical conditions.

Those whose Daimon is liberated know that the created world is holy and worthy of reverence. They know that human beings are all one species. They know that the survival of the species depends on the survival of its individual members and the survival of the other species that shape the ecology of our planet.

Four Legged Teachers

One of the great joys which spirited imagination brings us is the recognition that we are constantly being confronted with the lessons we need to master and that our teachers appear in the unlikeliest forms. Ego would prefer to look upon learning as a phenomenon occurring in formal institutions and presided over by other humans who have mastered their preferred fields of study.

Certainly, instructors in schools do impart essential learning but there are wise ones who say Earth itself is a school and that the things of the Earth teach the Soul just as educators teach the intellect.

From the earliest times shamanic people and humans who live close to Nature have looked upon animals as teachers. Their value in this regard is recognized in the Old Testament Book of Job (12:7-8) where we read:

> "If you would learn more, ask the cattle,
>   seek information from the birds of the air.
> The creeping things of earth will give you lessons,
>   and the fishes of the sea will tell you all."

With horse farming as an avocation I have lived very close to animals for many years and have learned much of value from observing them. Most touching is what I have learned from them about loss and death.

My wife and I have long tended a herd of Miniature Horses. This equine breed bears all the characteristics of its larger cousins but stands only 34 inches at the withers. They, along with our dogs, cats, and sundry other species have contributed immeasurably to my life.

Barring severe trauma, the horses consistently display an ability to bear pain and depart from life with a dignity and calmness that is enviable. Though the point is controversial, I would argue that they have an awareness of impending death but it is wonderful to observe how they live each day as fully as their condition allows right up until the moment they die.

Our original herd stallion, Caesar, is a shining example. He was a solid black stallion who displayed all the gallantry of a sixteen-hand stud. When he became afflicted with a neurological ailment we had to restrict his activities while attempting to establish a medical diagnosis and, hopefully, treatment for his condition. This meant he could no longer adhere to his usual routine of being turned out to pasture with his group of brood mares each morning.

Although obviously sick, Caesar did not for a moment shirk his duty. He took up a stately position beside the fence and watched those mares in the pasture throughout the day. At evening, he insistently called them in for feeding and they responded with hasty hoof-beats.

Given the limitations posed by his illness, he continued to do what he could do and did it without rancor. One could not observe his still proud carriage and think of him as a victim.

Sadly, his condition deteriorated and further suffering could not be justified. When the veterinarian came to put him down, we found him at his post of vigilance beside the fence. He took his last breath on that spot, being a good herd stallion until the end.

The little horse did not flinch at the lethal injection. He just sighed heavily and let go. He let go of everything familiar and dear to him more easily than I let go of him.

I buried him right there on his post. Like many of our animal graves, that little section of earth has earned the designation "sacred ground." Whenever I walk near it, the image of him standing and gazing out on his mares comes into my consciousness.

The Meanest Teacher And The Hardest Lesson

Sooner or later in life we must learn about death. Sooner or later we must die. The Daimon does not avoid this reality though our own death and the death of those we love is nearly unimaginable.

A client once told me she didn't want to love anyone because it would only lead to eventual separation and the pain would not be worth it. She has a point.

One way or another, we are destined to depart from our loved ones. This woman cannot imagine anything wonder-full about that experience.

I can empathize with her. Death is the meanest teacher of all and loss through Death is the hardest lesson. It is a class which none of us are allowed to skip. Some of us are required to take it early and some escape it until fairly late but the course is required.

I received my Great Lesson in loss when I was thirty years old and thought of Death as a happening in a galaxy far away. At that time, Shirley, my childhood sweetheart and marriage partner for five years, fell ill with acute leukemia. I was suddenly thrust into the role of standing helplessly by as she grew daily more pale and weak. When we would say goodnight at the hospital, I would stop at the door and wave on my way out. From her bed she would smile bravely and wave back.

Then, one night - the last night - I waved and saw that she could barely raise her hand. The next day she went into a coma. The day after that, she died.

She was pretty, intelligent, and eager to live. And she died.

Talk about your victims! My perception of myself as victim overshadowed the true victimization, which was Shirley's.

I was flooded with feelings of persecution. God had played a dirty trick on me and I hated him/her. The person around whom I had built all my hopes and dreams was snatched away. I wallowed in self-pity and excused it as part of my grief.

I did grieve deeply for my young wife but I was also full of rage. How dare "they" let this happen to me? I remained stuck in that anger for more than a year.

Eventually, a small inner voice (my Daimon) told me I should seek a message in Shirley's death. I resisted. If there were a lesson, it could not in a million years be profound enough to mitigate the pain of that lost life.

In spite of me, the lesson finally came through and, as I had predicted, it seemed trite. I didn't realize at the time how much my life would be directed by it.

What was this great truth? It sounds laughable as I put it into words. It is so goddam simple!

What is, is. That is the message. That is the great truth I learned from coping with my wife's death.

With the passage of time, I developed an appreciation and finally a reverence for its meaning. I could choose to stamp my feet and moan and groan forever about Shirley's death or any other loss in my life. I could even blow my brains out. It wouldn't change a thing. What is, is and what is, is an evolving and unfolding universe of which I am not in charge.

Buddha's teachings about attachment resounded in my mind. I was warring with the essence of life. Buddha taught it long ago: impermanence is the essence of life.

When I finally "got it," I could see that I had been acting out an irrational demand that God or any other Power Being should put everything back like it was. The workings of the universe should proceed according to my dictates.

The energy and consciousness I knew as the person Shirley had been transformed. Instead of searching for her in her new form, I had been seeking to get her back in her old form. Ironically, during the period I continued to insist on that, I had no reassuring feeling of contact with her.

During that angry, self-pitying year, I had recurrent dreams of Shirley being kept away from me by her family and others. In those dreams I searched for her and caught glimpses of her but something or someone always blocked access to her. In time, I recognized these barriers as symbols of my own refusal to meet her anew as Spirit.

In the end I let go of my demand that she be given back in the form I had known and loved. I decided to seek joy in relating to her as Spirit.

At that point, images of her in her new form began to appear to me. My memories and images of her as a dying person faded. Instead, she began to appear in my imagination as a laughing, lively spirit from another realm.

In my dreams, she was resurrected and we visited. During one very moving dream encounter she spoke in soft tones and told me everything was all right with her and I believed her. She informed me that she would have told me that much sooner had I been willing to listen.

My thoughts about Shirley have long since ceased to be obsessive or a source of anguish but I have not passed a day without experiencing a sense of contact with her. She is a constant, consoling presence in my inner world.

The client of whom I told you thought it not worthwhile to love and ultimately be deprived of love. She was unwilling to accept the temporary nature of all things and the rugged fragility of living creatures. She failed to recognize, as did I at one time, that form changes but nothing is lost.

There is but one precious moment in which anything exists as it is. That moment is now.

The lesson of love and loss leaves us aware that the greatest expression of love is letting go. It is in this act that the joy and pain of wonder become one.

> Sweet babe on my arm, I'll sing you a song
> and keep you from harm, but I won't hold you long.
> These moments so few to you may seem slow,
> but I promise you that I'll soon let you go.
>
> For now, let us rock and dream our sweet dreams
> while chimes of the clock count sun and moonbeams,
> and when you awake, save one kiss to throw.
> That's all that I'll take for my letting you go.
>
> This bond that we feel will not be a chain.
> This time that we steal will not come again.
> You'll soar like a dove and glance back below
> on my act of love which is letting you go.

CHAPTER FIFTEEN

The Secret Of The Gleam

> For thro' the Magic
> Of him the Mighty,
> Who taught me in childhood,
> There on the border
> Of boundless Ocean,
> And all but in Heaven
> Hovers the Gleam.
>
> > - Alfred Tennyson
> > Merlin and the Gleam

How shall we categorize the experiences we encounter when we turn ourselves over to spirited imagination? Are they nonsense? Are they psychological revelations? Are they mystical experiences?

My answer is "yes" to all of the above. They are non-sense in terms of the rational, linear kind of thinking we have been taught to value and trust. They are in-depth excursions into the psyche. They take place in a theater which is open to non-physical beings and environments and involve images of both.

It is this admixture which makes the Daimonic encounter unique and intimately nurturing for Soul while it is in its state of inseparability from the body and other components of the personality. As a result of this nurture Soul may expand and eventually at some point sufficiently detach to participate in a traditional, classical mystical experience.

Such experiences have been chronicled since antiquity and are identifiable by certain very consistent characteristics. These include:

1. The subject is unable to describe or has great difficulty in reporting the experience in words.

2. The subject feels changed by the experience in some significant way.
3. The subject is profoundly awed by the experience and may feel disoriented or on the brink of insanity.
4. The subject is left in an ecstatic mood.
5. The subject is left with a sense of having gained important new knowledge or an understanding of some great mystery.
6. The subject's sensations are heightened and/or hallucinations are experienced.
7. Great mythological themes such as death, rebirth, spirit encounters, magical powers, union with the Divine, etc. are woven into the content of the experience.
8. The subject's conceptual thinking remains intact.

As you see from this list, elements of a classical mystical experience are present to a greater or lesser extent in spirited imagination but they are usually intermingled with intrapsychic encounters, problem solving functions, and dialogue with archetypal images.

A degree of dissociation occurs when an individual is intensely focused on the images generated by spirited imagination but the subject is usually readily able to return to ordinary consciousness at will. Some clients express the feeling of having been visited by entities from outside of their individual personality but the locus of the encounter is nearly always perceived to be internal, i.e. a mental experience as opposed to an occurrence involving someone or something actually existing in the external environment as is the case with genuine hallucinations.

Unlike strict psychotherapeutic procedure, Daimonic work is psychospiritual inasmuch as Soul and Spirit are actively recognized as participants at all levels of the work and, at the top level, leadership is turned over to the Daimon or Guiding Spirit. The approach emphasizes the spiritual nature of the work without utilizing the trappings of any denominational religion. How, where and if the client wants to connect his/her spiritual growth with institutionalized worship is a matter of personal decision, respected but not brought into the work setting. Reading from scripture, praying, or engaging in religious rituals with clients is not part of the practice.

Traveling With The Daimon

Journey is the best metaphor for the psychic events which occur when we open up to spirited imagination. The structure of this book is modeled on the concept of journey.

We began in the remote corners of caves inhabited by our ancient ancestors. The paintings they left on the walls there attest to their recognition of the "something more" which is the foundation of our sense of wonder just as it was theirs. The cave paintings represent their effort to participate in the world beyond that of space, time, energy, and matter.

From their origin among the cave people, we followed the shamans, the first wizards to be set apart from their peers. Their recognition and use of a personality component which moved back and forth between the material and spiritual worlds to enhance healing, acquire wisdom, promote creativity, and commune with the Divine embodies the utilization of a power entity which the Greeks would later call the "Daimon."

We accompanied the shamans on their evolutionary path of transformation into magicians, priests. healers, saints, medical practitioners, and psychotherapists. We noted that, as their special abilities were recognized and accepted by the populous, individual members of clans, nations, and societies increasingly relied on the talents of these "specialists" and lost sight of their personal capacity for participating in the magic of the universe. Belief in that magic waned and became no longer culturally fashionable as the industrial revolution rolled around, bringing the supreme wonder called technology to center stage.

As a result of this evolution, most of us in the modern world lose touch with the Daimon in the process of growing up but not to the extent that we can't hear her beckoning from time to time. "Follow me," she says in that still, small voice which can be so compelling. "Follow me who follows the Gleam."

For accounts of those who have consciously made contact with the Daimon we have visited the realm of imagination as a separate reality. In the process we have discovered there is more to be learned about wonder from Dorothy of Oz, Don Quixote, Luke Skywalker, Alice of Wonderland, E.T., Harry Potter, and their kinsmen than from the most sophisticated research study.

We have seen how a meeting with the Daimon can occur through the unlikeliest sources: a passing hawk, the ghost of a dog, a boy in a gorilla suit, an abandoned radio, or an Oreo cookie. If we are willing to listen to and look at these and other phenomena generated by spirited imagination, they tell us that there is indeed "something more" to our lives than a "factual" analysis would suggest.

To travel with the Daimon is to enjoy and benefit from the power of wonder every day. Through continuous contact with her we remain constantly aware that we are surrounded by mystery and miracles. We sense a life force which resides within us and at the same time transcends us.

The Daimon enables us to take full advantage of the body/mind system's natural healing ability. She has eyes which are adapted for recognizing those who can teach us what we need to know and ears alert to their lessons. As we have observed, she is willing and able to receive information from such improbable sources as a woodpecker at work, a cuddly replica of Dumbo, a disembodied pair of hands, or a dying little horse.

We cannot walk far with the Daimon without developing a fresh appreciation of our own creativity and that of others. She helps us to see ourselves as intrinsic units in a created and creating universe. Creativity is the divine work of life and one of the many wonders in which we are free to participate.

No other part of our personality is as willing or able as the Daimon to get free from the constraints of the material world and travel to the mystical far horizons of inner and outer space. This ability is her special gift to the Soul.

Finally, the account of our sojourn with the Daimon becomes the mythic story of our existence. With and through her we can observe and enjoy the heroic aspects of our earthly journey. This answers a basic psychospiritual need for all of us: the need to find what relevance and meaning our lives have in the scheme of the vast panorama we call life.

Throughout our lifetimes most of us alternate between pursuing and fleeing from the Daimon. She draws us away from the material world in which we invest so much and points us toward the spiritual world in which we may place much hope but of which we are quite uncertain.

It is not so much our minds as our hearts which tell us the non-material world exists. We know about it primarily through activities that disengage us from our ordinary rational state of mind. We glimpse it most vividly when we are in altered states of consciousness such as a hypnotic trance; a prayerful, meditative state; during the performance of rituals; while suffering ordeals; when exploring silence; or as we give ourselves over to our imagination.

Who Does The Daimon Follow?

Once called forth the Daimon tends ceaselessly to urge us onward as if she has a specific destination in mind and a deadline for reaching it. She presents herself as a leader, yet we soon recognize that she is also being led.

Where and to what is she headed? What is her guiding principle?

For an answer we do well to return to Tennyson's (1899) poem about the archetypal Merlin who urges the young sailor to follow the Gleam. The Gleam is Tennyson's metaphor for the guiding principle of which we speak and the central metaphor of this book. Sooner or later, those of us who do Daimonic work want to know its secret meaning.

The aged and dying Merlin of the poem gives us a functional description of the Gleam by summarizing his enchanted career, emphasizing that the Gleam has been his guiding light ever since he learned the Magic from the Master. It has served, he recounts, to deliver him from dark and foreboding passages, to lead him to the wondrous places and creatures of the universe, to identify for him the pure and noble Arthur, and to illuminate life's dark shadows.

Clearly, for Merlin, pursuit of the elusive Gleam has left in its wake fulfillment and peace of soul, though as an entity it has remained essentially unreachable. Finally, in the twilight of his life, he sees it hovering on the border of the boundless Ocean which symbolizes the mysterious Unconscious, the unknown sea from which we arose and to whose depths we must surely return.

There the Gleam rests, all but in Heaven, taking up its position as an interface between the material and spiritual worlds. It is the bridge between the human and the Divine. It must be crossed in order for its meaning to be fully realized.

The message is that the Gleam is the ultimate wonder in a universe of wonders. It is the source of energy that makes all other wonders possible. It can be completely integrated only at the end of the journey.

The work of the Daimon, assigned to guide and protect us throughout life is complete only when she has delivered us to the threshold of the Gleam. With our last breath, that threshold is crossed.

Seeking The Name Of The Gleam

By calling forth his Daimon, a client named Roger discovered the secret of the Gleam just as countless pilgrims had done before him. Though a prosperous man, highly successful in the restaurant business, his alcoholism and abusiveness toward his wife when drinking had cost him his marriage. A few years later after attaining sobriety he sat in my office trying to figure out what was missing in his life.

I encouraged him to think about the last time he had experienced wonder. The question intrigued him but he could not recall any such occasion. He acknowledged that a lot of his memories were lost in the haze of his alcoholism.

We ended our session agreeing it would be worthwhile for him to think about the wonder issue. I promised to show him how to elicit the help of his Daimon at our next session if nothing came to him.

When he returned the following week, Roger brought with him a notebook and identified it as his "homework journal." It bore an entry describing a vivid memory which had come to him during his introspection. This is his account.

"For a while, all I could think about in regard to wonder was my personal accomplishments in starting a chain of restaurants and how much money I had made but, strangely, none of that gave me any sense of wonder at all. What I thought was magical about it was just my alcoholic glow. It was my self-centered little enterprise. Sure I gained wealth and some prestige but I didn't contribute much of anything to another single human being.

"Then, out of nowhere, came this memory of a particular event of some twelve years ago. I hadn't thought of it in ages. It involved my son, Larry, who was nine at the time.

"For some unknown reason I had eased up on my drinking a bit when he was that age and became more aware of him. God knows I wasn't much of a parent to either of my kids but for this brief period I started to pay attention to him. Maybe I was taken by his obvious striving for manhood by trying to be all boy.

"That stage of development reminded me of my own preadolescent years. I remembered how much I had wished my dad would do things with me - show me the ropes, so to speak. What a pipe dream that was! I found out later he didn't even believe I was his child.

"I'll never forget how Larry's eyes lit up when I told him that he and I were going to take an overnight fishing trip the following week. It would be our first fishing trip ever.

"He quickly checked a sudden rush of enthusiasm. I'm sure he assumed I wouldn't keep the promise. I had failed promises many times before.

"To my own surprise and his I did follow through. We got up early, put our gear in the car and went to the river. We rented camping space and a boat and putted off to the inlets like Jim and Huck. I got to know more about my little boy that day than at any time before or since. I discovered he was bright, funny, enthusiastic, and very pleased to have a dad, even if only for a week-end.

"We only caught three fish. Larry got two to my one. They were pretty small, besides.

"Landlubbers that we were, we got the propeller tangled in some underwater grass and had to go over the side of the boat to free it. We felt like rugged rangers slogging along in the waist deep water. When

I got the motor going again, Larry gave me a salute and called me 'Captain.'

"My son listened fascinated beside our campfire as I told him tales about my own boyhood. Some of them were lies.

"For example, I was a punter on my high school football team and only got in for a few plays in my entire career. That's probably because I couldn't kick worth a damn.

"I told Larry I pulled several games out of the fire with outstanding punts. I'll never forget how he looked at me and said, 'I'll bet you were one tough dude, Dad.'

"He was proud of me and he was proud of our catch. We pan fried the fish and opened a can of beans to go with them. I can still taste that little feast as I write about it.

"My heart swelled as I watched Larry eat those fishes. I knew I was sharing in one of those ordinary but great moments in his life. I felt wonderful about having helped him to create it. God gave us the beautiful day and the fish but, for once, I had also given Larry something - myself.

"I promised him we would go fishing more regularly after that but, of course, defaulted. It wasn't long before he, my daughter, and their mother were out of my life. They eventually moved out of state and I stopped hearing from them. I felt hurt and angry but made no special effort to reestablish contact.

"Larry has no reason to think about me much but I know in my heart that he remembers that fishing trip just as I do. I wouldn't trade a moment of it even though it involved lies and broken promises. It was the most I could give to anyone at that time. It's a sad commentary but for once I was doing my best.

"That, dear therapist, is my day of wonder. For a few hours I was a real magician."

The Gleam settled over this precious memory and, after a little more self discovery, Roger decided to follow it. He knew there were lots of little boys in the world needing and seeking the magic of a man to man relationship. He could not salvage his relationship with Larry but he recognized that he had participated in the Magic on one glorious occasion and that he could do it again.

Roger has become enthusiastically involved in the Big Brothers organization and today is creatively giving himself to appreciative youngsters. He is following the Gleam. His name for the Gleam is "doing the right thing."

Embedded in his story is a lesson that applies to all of us. We cannot effectively pursue the Gleam until we recognize and take charge of the dark side of our personality. At some point, the Daimon almost always introduces into consciousness elements of our Shadow, the part of us that we disclaim or disown - the thoughts, feelings, and behaviors which we think are unacceptable and leave unacknowledged.

The Daimon will not allow us to be naive about our true nature. He knows there is an element of evil in each of us that would lead us down a path of defeat and destructiveness if allowed. His choice to be guided by a higher source offers some assurance that our dark side will not triumph but if we will it strongly enough we can turn him away from the Gleam.

Yet, even as we support the Daimonic quest, the pursuit of the Gleam demands that we pass through the dark side, not around it. We journey with our Shadow whether it is acknowledged or not. We must integrate the most distasteful parts of ourselves in order to be whole. We cannot be holy without being whole.

A Clue To The Final Destination

In using journey as a metaphor, we cannot ignore the idea of destination or direction. Yes, we may experience more growth from the travel than the arrival but we are not talking about a random excursion. Tennyson's Merlin reached that point where the Gleam hovered and so shall we. .

We know when we shall reach that place which is perhaps more of a state than a place. It comes at the end of our earthly life. But what shall we call it?

Dorothy in The Wizard of Oz (Baum, 1944) has marvelous adventures and establishes loving relationships in the enchanted land of Oz but her longing throughout the story is to return home. The lovable little alien from outer space in Steven Spielberg's film, E.T.

The Extra-Terrestrial (Universal, 1982) finds himself in similar circumstances.

We empathize with these fictional space travelers because we identify with them. At times we also feel that we are on alien shores far from home.

We grow weary of our earthly sojourn. Despite the wonders, despite the comedy, adventure, and drama of life, there are times when we wish we had just been allowed to remain at home in the first place.

Some say that returning home and staying there is a privilege human beings must earn. This model designates Earth as a school wherein we learn what we must master to be entitled to that blissful state of remaining permanently at home. Through a series of lives we are constantly refined until we reach a level of completeness that qualifies us to graduate.

Some say that a house of many mansions awaits us for permanent residence as soon as our life task is complete. Regardless of the imagined particulars, it is for home that we are headed, the ground from which we sprung. The place where we were known before we were born.

We return home the same as when we left but enriched and expanded by our earthly experience. I received a beautiful lesson on this subject just recently.

Though our ranch is twenty-five miles from the Gulf beaches I discovered within its confines a perfectly intact and beautiful whelk shell. Undoubtedly, it had found its way inland in a load of fill but I don't know how to account for its state of preservation.

Suddenly, irresistibly, there it was in my path. I could not bring myself to walk over or around it. Its presence was too strange and wonderful. This skeleton of an animal belonging to the sea had found its way twenty-five miles inland to the exact spot on which I was about to step. In the ordinary scheme of things it was an encounter most unlikely ever to occur.

I picked it up. Its colors were a bit faded but it still radiated some of its full glory. I found myself wishing I could return it to life.

Holding it in my hand, I discovered it was warm from the sun. Then, I smelled it and held it to my ear, discovering it was still able to deliver to my senses the essence of its salt water home.

At that point, I became amused with myself for wishing it life. Its creature spirit, its essence, was still very much alive.

Tucking it in my pocket, I thought about its strange odyssey. It had come a long and improbable way to reach the hands of someone who appreciated its beauty and meaning. I think the meeting was no accident.

I believe the shell came to me as a messenger, arriving in a landlocked universe totally alien to its aquatic environment. If whelks have imagination I'm sure it could never have imagined such a place.

It suggested to me that our ultimate destination may well be some place of which we, like the whelk, know absolutely nothing and can not imagine. Yet, it is a place where we shall be recognized, accepted, and loved for what we bring to it of the life we have lived.

The place over which the Gleam hovers is our home. It is the place where we are known.

The Name Of The Gleam Revealed

Those who have sought the Gleam through the ages have named its secret with surprising constancy. That secret name has echoed through the corridors of time where it has been remembered, forgotten, and remembered again.

Its name is ancient and it has remained unchanged by all the history that has passed before us. Its name is Love.

This love is something far beyond human love, which is erratic at best. It is Pure Love, the Source of Love. It is the Light. It is another name for God. It is the most powerful of all the forces that we recognize.

The Gleam is a projection of this higher dimension of love. It is the magnet which draws us back again and again to the quest for that which is purer, finer, nobler, more glorious than anything we have known.

It is the force behind our movements as we do the Dance of Life in tempo with the unique rhythms of our own inner music. We all participate in the dance and it is different for each of us.

Some of us do our steps for a long time while others make but a brief appearance on the floor. Some of us move about vigorously with passion or frenzy while others proceed slowly and methodically. Some display artfulness or elegance while others prefer to perform with humor or vulgarity.

There are those who dance alone, those who dance in pairs, and those who dance in ensemble. For many of us it takes a long while to discover that our idiosyncratic way of dancing ultimately conceals or expresses that propelling energy of life we call love.

Love is within us as well as over the horizon. We are love seeking Greater Love.

With the Daimon as our guide we pursue Love, not just the things we love but what we are and what we are becoming through the power of love. Like other wonders, love demands a great deal of us. Like other wonders, it requires our active participation.

Love is the secret of the Gleam. The Gleam draws us to those places where love awaits to be given or received. It draws us to those stark, cold places where the seed of love needs to be planted.

It draws us to those places where we can participate in the loving act of creation. It takes us where we are needed to fulfill the promise of love and, at the same time, to be fulfilled.

The Gleam beckons us to become whole through, with, and by love. That is the holy state to which we are called.

In a much-quoted statement from scripture Jesus clearly emphasizes the importance of wholeness. Note his pointedly repetitive underscoring of the word "all" in this passage from Luke (10:27-29):

"You must love the lord your God with all your heart, with all your soul, with all your strength, and with all your mind, and your neighbor as yourself."

We cannot give our "all" when we are out of touch with who we are. We may not be destined ever to make our Unconscious completely conscious but, as we strive to do so, we grow in love, understanding, humility, and compassion. This is the reward of responding to the call to be whole.

And there you have it. The magic is that which we have known from evolutionary infancy and keep forgetting. It is all around us, all inside of us. It is a given.

The magic is not a skill to be learned. It is a wonder in which to participate.

It is our human nature to desire signs of the Love of which I speak. By looking through the Daimon's eye we find them in abundance.

A new wonder was recently created in the soft branches of an elm tree near our house. Seemingly out of nowhere a beehive appeared with its busy inhabitants constantly going and coming.

Popular knowledge tells us that, inside the hive, scout bees are frequently performing an incredible series of movements called a dance which instructs their fellow gatherers regarding the precise flight pattern to follow to find nectar which is too distant to be readily located by smell or sight. This remarkable feat alone identifies the bee as a mystical creature.

I looked upon the bees as a gift of love from a source beyond my understanding. The force that guided them led them to choose my tree in front of my window to build their heart shaped home.

I sought to hear their message. Were these honey makers harbingers of a new "sweetness" about to emerge into my life? Had they brought their industriousness into my view to suggest that I become more or less busy in my daily routine? Had they, with their accomplishments that far exceed what their size and strength suggest is possible, entered my awareness to remind me that no task is insurmountable if the will is strong enough?

I listened to the humming of the bees and wondered if I was hearing the voice of God. Certainly, the questions they generated were ones I need to ask myself.

Shortly after that questioning provided me with the information I needed to glean from the bees, they were gone. They left abruptly. I looked out the window one morning and found an empty hive. Silently, quickly, and for reasons I could not begin to fathom, they had moved on.

I have missed that unit of creative, mystical life outside of my window. I'm not sure what if anything the bees needed from their stay with me but in terms of what I needed to learn from them our transaction was complete. I am reminded once again of the old truth that says, "when the student is ready to learn, the teacher appears."

The great love story goes on.

In his lesser known works, <u>Sylvie and Bruno</u> and <u>Sylvie and Bruno Concluded</u>, Lewis Carroll (1982) has given us a fairy story which includes as he says in his Preface, "some thoughts that may prove...not wholly out of harmony with the graver cadences of Life." Indeed, the books are filled with worthwhile thoughts on wonder, magic, and love. Perhaps you, like I, will want to take his thoughts along as you continue your quest for the Gleam:

> Say whose is the skill that paints valley and hill,
> Like a picture so fair to the sight?
> That flecks the green meadow with sunshine and shadow,
> Till the little lambs leap with delight?
> 'Tis a secret untold to hearts cruel and cold,
> Though, 'tis sung, by the angels above.
> In notes that ring clear for the ears that can hear -
> And the name of the secret is Love!

THE ROAD WINDS ON YET MORE

Norman G. Middleton, M.S.W.

APPENDIX:
A RELAXATION PROCEDURE FOR IMAGING

Relaxation facilitates inward focusing and enhances imagery. A brief relaxation procedure is recommended before you begin any imaging experience. The relaxation does not have to be deep, so only a few minutes are required.

The following is a set of suggestions to help you relax. They work best if you make a tape recording of them in your own voice or that of a trusted other. They can be used verbatim or modified in any way that makes them more effective for you. They should be recited slowly and clearly with significant pauses wherever you see a dash (-).

Before your imagery session, communicate to your Unconscious the kind of image you would like to receive, e.g., your Daimon, one of your sub-selves, a particular emotion, a dream image, etc. You may also make an open ended request, such as "send me an image that will help with my personal growth."

Take whatever steps are necessary to keep your imaging time uninterrupted. Then, get yourself comfortably situated and turn on your recording.

THE PROCEDURE

Take a deep breath and exhale slowly through your mouth - Notice the relaxation in your chest and abdomen as you breathe out -

Take a second deep breath and, once again, exhale slowly - Now take a third breath and as you exhale allow your eyes to close if they have not already done so - With your eyes comfortably closed, breathe normally and enjoy the quiet that surrounds you - There is nothing you have to do - You don't have to talk, or move, or make any effort of any kind - Just be right where you are, going deeper into a relaxed state.

Allow any tension anywhere in your body to flow out of you and away from you - Visualize it as a vapor that is flowing out of the tips of your fingers, the tips of your toes and the top of your head - Feel your muscles going loose and limp as the tension leaves your body - You have set in motion a process of physical relaxation that will proceed on its own as long as you do not interfere with it - Just let go and allow it to continue.

While you're becoming more and more deeply relaxed, allow your conscious mind to drift away from your immediate surroundings - You're going deeper and deeper inside of yourself - Just let go and let what happens happen - Anything outside of yourself is of no importance on this journey - It's like being on an escalator that's taking you slowly and gently to deeper and deeper levels of your being - The ride makes you feel far away, detached, and drowsy - The deeper you go, the more calm and peaceful you feel.

If you haven't already done so, notice the heavy feeling that is developing in your arms and legs - The muscles there have relaxed to such a degree that it feels like it would take a great effort to move an arm or a leg and it's nice to know you don't have to - You can just drowsily continue your pleasant ride, going deeper and deeper - Time is slowing down, giving you lots of time to go as deep as you wish.

When this relaxation procedure is complete, your interest will turn to some images that you have requested - They are being sent to help you learn, explore, heal, and grow - Be sure to accept without censorship whatever comes to you, no matter how strange or inappropriate it may seem.

For now, your body is relaxing, your mind is relaxing - In your relaxed state, all the systems of your body are working smoothly and efficiently - You can safely lose touch with your body along with everything else on the outside - You can be pure mind, ready to receive you helpful images and to work with them in whatever is best for you - You can float and drift and dream your images, floating like a leaf caught in the wind, drifting down, down, down, deeper and deeper.

Now allow your imagination to create for you a place in which you feel at one with your surroundings - When you feel fully in this place, noting all the sights, sounds, smells, tastes, and sensations it brings to you, find a comfortable spot and wait patiently until something captures your attention.

REFERENCES

Achterberg, Jeanne. IMAGERY IN HEALING. Boston: Shambhala, 1985.

Baum, L. Frank. THE WIZARD OF OZ. New York: Grosset & Dunlap, 1944.

Baumeister, Roy. EVIL: INSIDE HUMAN VIOLENCE AND CRUELTY.
New York: Freeman, 1999.

Blair, Lawrence. RHYTHMS OF VISION. New York: Schocken Books, 1976.

Campbell, Joseph. THE MASKS OF GOD: PRIMITIVE MYTHOLOGY. New York: Arkana, 1991.

Carroll, Lewis. THE WORKS OF LEWIS CARROLL. Giuliano, Edward (ed.). New York: Crown Publishers, 1982.

Cousins, Norman. THE ANATOMY OF AN ILLNESS AS PERCEIVED BY THE PATIENT. New York: Norton, 1979.

Donne, John. THE COMPLETE POETRY OF JOHN DONNE. Shawcros, John (ed.). New York: Doubleday and Co., 1967.

Dossey, Larry. HEALING WORDS: THE POWER OF PRAYER AND THE PRACTICE OF MEDICINE. New York: HarperCollins, 1993.

Eliade, Mircea. SHAMANISM: ARCHAIC TECHNIQUES OF ECSTACSY. Bollingen Series LXXVI. New York: Pantheon, 1964.

Foundation for Inner Peace. A COURSE IN MIRACLES. Tiburon, CA: Foundation for Inner Peace, 1975.

Gilbert, W. and Sullivan, A. THE WORKS OF SIR WILLIAM GILBERT AND SIR ARTHUR SULLIVAN. Roslyn, N.Y.: Black's Readers Service, 1937.

Harner, Michael. THE WAY OF THE SHAMAN. New York: Bantam Books, 1982.

Harrison, Edward. MASKS OF THE UNIVERSE. New York: Macmillan, 1985.

Homer. THE ILIAD OF HOMER. Pope, Alexander (trans.). New York: Macmillan, 1965.

Horowitz, Mardi. IMAGE FORMATION AND PSYCHOTHERAPY. New York: Aronson, 1983.

THE JERUSALEM BIBLE. Jones, Alexander (gen. ed.). New York: Doubleday & Co., 1968.

Kipling, Rudyard. COMPLETE VERSE. New York: Doubleday, 1989.

Lloyd, David. "Chuckles Bites the Dust" script for The Mary Tyler Moore Show, created by Allan Burns and James L Brooks. MTM Enterprises, Inc., 1975.

Maslow, Abraham. MOTIVATION AND PERSONALITY. New York: Harper, 1954.

Middleton, Norman. IMAGINATIVE HEALING. San Jose, CA: R&E Publishers, 1993.

_____. THE CAVERNS OF MY MIND. Bristol, IN: Wyndham Hall Press, 1985.

_____. "Letting You Go," and "When the Buddha Bells Ring Eventide." Unpublished poems.

Murchie, Guy. THE SEVEN MYSTERIES OF LIFE. Boston: Houghton Mifflin, 1981.

Plato. "Apology" in Five Great Dialogues. B. Jowett (trans.) and L. Loomis (ed.). New York: Walter Black, 1942.

Roberts, Bernadette. THE EXPERIENCE OF NO-SELF. Boston: Shambhala, 1982.

Rogers, Carl. CLIENT CENTERED THERAPY. Boston: Houghton Mifflin, 1951.

Samuels, Mike & Samuels, Nancy. SEEING WITH THE MIND'S EYE. New York: Random House, 1975.

Shakespeare, William. THE WORKS OF WILLIAM SHAKESPEARE COMPLETE. Roslyn, N.Y.: Black's Reader Service, 1937.

Stevenson, Robert L. THE STRANGE CASE OF DR. JEKYLL AND MR. HYDE. New York: Bantam, 1981.

_____. A CHILD'S GARDEN OF VERSES. Oxford: Oxford University Press, 1996.

Tennyson, Alfred. "Merlin and the Gleam," in THE POETIC AND DRAMATIC WORKS OF ALFRED LORD TENNYSON. New York: Houghton, Miflin and Co., 1899.

_____. IDYLLS OF THE KING. New York: Penguin Books, 1983.

Teresa of Avila. "The Interior Castle" in THE COLLECTED WORKS OF ST. TERESA OF AVILA. Vol. 2. Trans. by Kavanaugh, K. and Rodriguez, O. Washington, D.C.: ICS Publications, 1980.

Thompson, Francis. "The Hound of Heaven" in Aldington, R. (ed.) THE VIKING BOOK OF POETRY. New York: The Viking Press,
1941.

Vaughn, Henry. "They Are All Gone..." in Aldington, R. (ed.) THE VIKING BOOK OF POETRY. New York: The Viking Press, 1941.

Viorst, Judith. NECESSARY LOSSES. New York: Ballantine Books, 1986.

Watson, John. "Psychology as the Behaviorist Views It," Psychological Review, Vol. 20, pp. 158-77, 1913.

Whitman, Walt. LEAVES OF GRASS. New York: Doubleday and Co., 1940.

ABOUT THE AUTHOR

Norman Middleton is a Licensed Clinical Social Worker and Licensed Marriage and Family Therapist who has been engaged in the practice of psychotherapy for thirty-five years. He has presented workshops on using imagery for healing, personal growth, and spiritual development at the state and national levels. He is a Board Certified Diplomate in Clinical Social Work and is listed in WHO'S WHO IN AMERICA. He maintains a private counseling practice in Sarasota, Florida, where he spends his leisure time at the family's miniature horse ranch.